Weldon Rising & Disappear

This volume brings together two provocative, sexy and brutally comic plays from 'the finest playwright to have emerged in the 1990s'. *Financial Times*

Weldon Rising

Downtown New York. The temperature is soaring. In the meat-packing district, Natty Weldon's lover is casually butchered by a homicidal homophobe. The witnesses do not intervene. Natty flees in terror, two lesbians watch from their apartment window and a flamboyant transvestite prostitute cowers in the street below. But life changes for them all after the murder.

Disappeared

Sarah Casey, a travel agent who has never been anywhere, meets the mysterious Elston Rupp in a bar in New York's Hell's Kitchen. They walk out together and she is never seen again. Was she murdered, has she escaped from the city of loners, or has she simply disappeared?

Phyllis Nagy was born in New York City and now lives in London. Her work includes *Weldon Rising* (Royal Court Theatre and Liverpool Playhouse, 1992), *Trip's Cinch* (Actors Theatre of Louisville, 1994), an adaptation of Nathaniel Hawthorne's *The Scarlet Letter* (Denver Center Theatre Company, 1994), *Butterfly Kiss* (Almeida Theatre, 1994), the Mobil prize-winning *Disappeared* (Leicester Haymarket and Royal Court, 1995) and *The Strip* (Royal Court, 1995).

Butterfly Kiss
The Scarlet Letter
Trip's Cinch
The Strip

Phyllis Nagy

Weldon Rising
&
Disappeared

Methuen Drama

Methuen Drama **Modern Plays**

First published in Great Britain 1996
by Methuen Drama

Weldon Rising first published in October 1992 in *Plays International*;
and in 1994 by Methuen Drama in *Plays by Women: Ten*
Copyright © 1992, 1994, 1996 by Phyllis Nagy
Disappeared first published in 1995 by Samuel French Ltd
Copyright © 1995, 1996 by Phyllis Nagy
Lines from *London Fields* by Martin Amis quoted on page 4 by
permission of Jonathan Cape Ltd

The author has asserted her moral rights

ISBN 0–413–70150–6

A CIP catalogue for this book
is available from the British Library

Typeset by Wilmaset Ltd, Birkenhead, Wirral
Printed in Great Britain by Cox & Wyman Ltd, Reading, Berks

Caution

Contents

Weldon Rising

To Mel

*So if you ever felt something behind you, when you weren't even one,
like a welcome heat, like a bulb, like a sun, trying to shine right across
the universe – it was me. Always me. It was me. It was me.*
(Martin Amis)

Weldon Rising was first produced by the Royal Court Theatre in association with the Liverpool Playhouse. The play opened at the Liverpool Playhouse Studio on 27 October 1992. The first London performance was at the Royal Court Theatre Upstairs on 3 December 1992, with the following cast:

Natty Weldon	Simon Gregor
Marcel	Andrew Woodall
Tilly	Melee Hutton
Jaye	Rosie Rowell
Jimmy	Paul Viragh
Boy	Matthew Wait

Directed by Penny Ciniewicz
Designed by Ruari Murchison
Lighting by Jon Linstrum

Characters

Natty Weldon, *35. Distressed by his ordinary good looks. Adrift, guilty, obsessive. However, his self-effacing sense of humour enables him to fight rather than crumble.*
Tilly, *not quite 30, but older than she'd like to be. Pretty enough, which is problematic for her. Naturally curious and incongruously romantic.*
Jaye, *not quite 30. Very fit, clean and thoroughly gorgeous. Mean, caustic and not afraid of being unsympathetic. Not at all coy or girlish, but not butch either.*
Marcel, *stunning young transvestite without a permanent address. Very much a man. Not at all effeminate or mincing.*
Jimmy, *Natty's lover. He's everything Natty isn't: tall, beautiful, outspoken.*
Boy, *so beautiful and dangerous that no two people can remember him in quite the same way. Very young and unfailingly polite, even when violent. The sum of all fears.*

The Setting
Little West 12th Street, a cobbled back street in New York
City's meat-packing district. Factory buildings that may or
may not be deserted. Shadowy, all of it. One surface must be
covered entirely by a detailed map of the meat-packing
district. The map is enormous, overwhelming. One area of
the stage, preferably above street level, represents Tilly and
Jaye's apartment during the first several scenes of the play.
The apartment should not be represented naturalistically.
What's important is the sense that the women watch Natty
and Marcel from a separate space. It is the hottest evening of
the year.

Note
The music should be treated as an integral part of the text
rather than as background noise. Therefore, it is especially
important that the versions of the songs indicated are used in
production.
   Much of the punctuation used in the play is not standard
and is intended to create a non-naturalistic pattern to the
language. The play works best in performance when strict
attention is paid to the specifics of the punctuation.
Similarly, the use of capitals in some lines does not
necessarily indicate an increase in volume; rather, it is meant
to indicate shifts in thought.

Lights up on **Natty Weldon**. *He's in the street. He wears boxer shorts and a wool beret. He sits before an art deco vanity, the surface of which is covered by bottles of cologne. The vanity's mirror is pasted over with postcards. Open boxes scattered about. Clothes overflowing from them. A portable steel clothing rack, full of men's stuff. There is a walkman and two tiny speakers set up on one edge of the vanity.* **Natty** *douses himself with cologne from every bottle.*

Lights up on **Marcel**. *He wears something ridiculous, like a plastic dress and platform shoes, but looks dazzling nonetheless. He is meticulously washing out a pair of pantyhose in a ceramic basin.*

Natty I might have been beautiful. I think. In Morocco. Ann Arbor. Montreal. San Francisco. Brisbane. Detroit. In transit. I used to be a little beautiful in transit.

Marcel Marcel says: you were never beautiful. Marcel says: you're a liar. Marcel says: YOU STINK.

Natty *switches on the walkman. It's Led Zeppelin's 'Trampled Underfoot'.* **Natty** *begins to unpack the boxes, hanging the clothing on the rack.*

Marcel Marcel says: shut that shit off. Marcel says: SHUT THAT SHIT OFF.

Lights up on **Tilly** *and* **Jaye**. *They observe the scene from their apartment.* **Tilly** *drinks beer and eats popcorn, totally fascinated by the proceedings. Empty beer bottles are scattered around them.*

Tilly He's very skinny. Arms like twigs. That's unhealthy.

Jaye I despise men with skinny arms.

Tilly We should feed him. Maybe.

Jaye He's way past the stage for feeding. Forget it.

Marcel Marcel is displeased. Marcel wants some quietude in which to wash her tights.

Natty *ignores* **Marcel** *and continues unpacking clothes.* **Marcel** *hurls the walkman and speakers onto the street. Music out.*

Marcel Marcel detests rock and roll. And queer boys who smell of marzipan.

Natty   That was Jimmy's favourite. I used to be beautiful.
A little. With Jimmy.

Lights down on **Natty** *and* **Marcel**.

Tilly   Men are violent. Even when they wear dresses. Let's
stay home forever.

Jaye *kisses the back of* **Tilly**'s *neck while* **Tilly** *continues to observe
the unseen scene.*

Jaye   Hold still and let me bite your neck.

Tilly   It's too fucking hot for that. Do we have any more
beer? I drink too much beer.

Jaye   You don't drink enough. You're coherent when you're
drunk.

Tilly   It's a hundred and twenty degrees and if I don't have
another beer I'm gonna . . . ouch. Stop that. You're hurting
me.

Jaye   When you're drunk, you let me bite your neck.

Tilly   You know, he's really very skinny. But he has a nice
ass. WOULD YOU PLEASE STOP MAULING ME.

Jaye   Sorry. No more beer. We're dry.

Tilly   Liar. You're hoarding it. Under the floorboards.

Jaye   Tough. No sex, no booze.

Tilly   I can't believe you're doing this to me. It's blackmail.

Jaye   Hey. These are the rules. I bite your neck, you get a
beer. I rip off your clothes, you get another beer.

Tilly   Don't be such a boy.

Jaye   Listen to yourself. Since when did you decide to be
celibate?

Tilly   Since it's gotten so hot I can't think straight. Jesus. I
need a drink. Please.

Jaye   Bulldyke.

Tilly   Flattery just won't work any more, honey. Look. That silly drag queen is washing his pantyhose.

Jaye   You've been at that window for weeks. Talk to me, Tilly.

Tilly   I wonder what size he wears. I hate my name. It's withered. We got any more popcorn?

Jaye   Pay some attention to me or I'll get another girlfriend.

Tilly   I bet he wears queen-sized. Long legs. Yeah. Well. Who are you kidding? Nobody else would have you. You're a mess.

Jaye   Fuck off.

Tilly   No, really. You're worse than me. And you got no booze in the house, no food and you got no air-conditioning. Why don't we have air-conditioning?

Jaye   I like the heat. It's unpleasant.

Tilly   And why does this skinny little fuck keep packing and unpacking clothes? I mean, why doesn't he just trash them?

Jaye   I'm out of here.

Tilly   Oh yeah? Where you going?

Jaye   I told you. I'm on the prowl.

Tilly   I hate it when you're pathetic.

Jaye   Okay. So I might be persuaded to stay home and hook you up to a beer i.v.

Tilly   Don't go out.

Jaye   Why not? I look good under lampposts. Cheap and sexy. That's me.

Tilly   You might lose your keys. Then what. Then you'd be lost to the streets.

Jaye turns **Tilly** *towards her*.

Jaye   You ought to get out, too. Come with me.

Tilly   I can't. My hair's dirty. I smell.

Jaye   Tilly. It's all right to go outside now. It's all over.

Tilly   We should have helped him. We should have run out into the street then.

Jaye   I'm not listening to this any more.

Tilly   Why didn't we help him? Now look at him. Nearly naked and still trying to hide his bald spot.

Jaye *holds out a beer to* **Tilly**, *as if from nowhere*.

Jaye   Whoops. Look what I found. It's a . . . Corona.

Tilly   I knew you were holding out on me. Bitch. Give it here.

Jaye   Fuck me first.

Tilly   Were you always this mean?

Jaye   Yup. Now. What's it gonna be?

Tilly   We used to be civilized, you know.

Jaye   Too late for that. I'll count to ten. One. Two.

Tilly   I can't help this, Jaye. I can't. We watched a man die and I can't move now. I want to sit at the window and rot. And drink till I drop.

Jaye   Three. Four. I swear, when I get to ten, this all goes down the drain. Five. Six.

Tilly   For chrissakes. Just let me have the fucking beer, all right?

Jaye   Seven. Eight.

Tilly   Okay. OKAY. STOP. What do you want? I'll do it.

Jaye   On your knees.

Tilly *drops to her knees.* **Jaye** *goes to her, opens the beer.*

Jaye   Mouth open, head tilted back.

Tilly *complies.* **Jaye** *feeds beer to* **Tilly**.

Jaye   We did what we could. We called the cops. We're not responsible.

Tilly   Just . . . shut up and feed me.

Jaye *bends to kiss* **Tilly**.

Jaye   What do you love more: me or booze?

Tilly   Shut up. Feed me.

Jaye *kisses* **Tilly**. *Lights down on them. Lights up on* **Natty**. *He cuts his toe-nails.*

Natty   One night's like the next. I'm indecisive. I don't know which tie to wear. I can't choose between Chinese takeout or pizza. I think if I cut long and hard enough my feet will bleed and I won't be able to go out. We'll have to stay home, but no. Jimmy's ready to go and I can't stop him. We argue. I choose my most unfashionable tie, hoping he'll be embarrassed to be seen with me. But no. We go. We leave the apartment. We're on the street. We're moving.

Jimmy *enters*.

Jimmy   It'll be good for you. Get out and meet your peers.

Natty   They're not my peers. I own a small business. I have customers. I'm not political. They're your peers.

Jimmy   Dances are fun, Natty. Not political.

Natty   You can dance. I can't. You know I look like Peter Lorre in *M* when I dance.

Jimmy   You have no gay friends.

Natty   I'm not good-looking enough to have gay friends. You go. I'll go home and bake muffins. But please, Jimmy, don't make me go to a dance where I'll meet lots of boys who can't have sex, looking to have it anyway.

Jimmy   You've become so unfair in your old age. A shame. Come on. Have fun with me. Like in the old days.

Natty   Every day of my life is an old day.

Jimmy   Natty, everybody knows you're queer. Even your . . . customers.

Natty   Who told you that?

Jimmy   You don't fool anybody. Besides, it's not like we skip down the avenue holding hands and singing Judy Garland songs.

Natty   I don't see any reason to broadcast my sexuality.

Jimmy   Yeah, yeah. I know this story already.

Natty   Really. In fifteen years have you learned nothing about me? I'm discreet.

Jimmy   You're invisible.

Natty   I think you need drugs. Valium.

Jimmy   Maybe I'd like to hold your hand. Walk along Eighth Avenue and spit at passers-by.

Natty   You spit. I'll crawl under a manhole. Jimmy: I DON'T WANT TO GO. I don't do witty repartee. I sell lamps. I sometimes wear polyester. I can't dance and leather makes me squeamish. I don't vote. I don't go to bars. My only friends are miserably unhappy straight girls who hover in cabarets. We sing along to every show tune ever written and weep at last call. I've never done a popper in my life. I just . . . do you. Come home and watch *Now Voyager* with me.

Jimmy   I need people. Music. Smoke-filled rooms.

Natty   Fine. I'll smoke a carton of Camels for you. Just come home. With me.

Jimmy   Be more dangerous for me.

Natty   Love me for my cowardice.

Jimmy   I've done that for fifteen years. It's time for a change.

Natty   I'm allergic to change.

Jimmy   We haven't been out as a couple in ages. The boys don't believe me when I say I have a lover. You ought to prove I'm not a liar.

Natty   But I *am* a liar. I'm pathological. I lie about everything. I crave it.

Jimmy   I've got to be with people. Men. Happy sweaty men. Pressed together. Dancing for joy.

Natty   On the train this morning, I was reading something German. Told the sexy kid next to me that I was taking a PhD in German literature. Told him it was the wave of the future. He was impressed. Gave me his phone number. Would you like his number? I bet *he* dances.

Jimmy   I don't want a catalogue of your lies.

Natty   When I met you, I told you my mother was Sonja Henje. That she dropped me out on the ice in the middle of a double toe-loop.

Jimmy   I thought it was a lovely image. I still do.

Natty   If I lie enough, it keeps me healthy. But in order to lie successfully, one can't participate too much. In life.

Jimmy   There's nothing wrong with selling lamps, Nathaniel.

Natty   You call me Nathaniel when you're angry with me. You've called me that a lot lately. The thing about lamps is, as you get older, it's less and less flattering to bathe yourself in light. I replaced all the bulbs in the shop with 40-watters.

Jimmy   I won't indulge you.

Natty   And another thing. I'm really fat. Yesterday I gained twenty pounds when you weren't looking.

Boy *enters. He lights a cigarette, watches them. They watch him.*

Jimmy   My God. Remember when you looked like that?

Natty   I never looked like that.

Jimmy   What a face.

Natty   Sure. It's not dropped yet. Wait ten years and oh
. . . a few hundred thousand cigarettes later.

Jimmy   He smokes like he's waiting to be fucked.

Natty   No doubt he is. Waiting. For sure.

Jimmy   Are you jealous?

Natty   I'm not in a position to be jealous. People like me
are grateful for any attention paid to us. We're happy for
crumbs. Morsels.

Jimmy   You're jealous. It's fantastic. Come on. Let's go.

Jimmy *holds out his hand to* **Natty**. **Natty** *doesn't take it.*

Jimmy *smiles at* **Boy**.

Jimmy (*to* **Boy**)   Excuse us. We do this all the time.

Boy   What? What do you do all the time?

Jimmy   Argue in public.

Boy   I wasn't listening.

Natty   All right. You win. Let's go. I'll cringe in a corner
and watch you dance.

Boy   Have you got the correct time?

Natty   I . . . you talking to me?

Boy   Yes. The time. What is it?

Natty   It's . . . late. I don't know.

Boy   Don't you have a watch?

Natty   Oh God. Don't hurt me.

Jimmy   Natty . . .

Boy   Hey. Fuck off asshole. I asked you for the time. That's
all.

Jimmy   It's 10.45.

Boy   Oh yeah? Where you going?

Natty   That's really none of your business.

Boy   Are you a faggot?

Jimmy   Come on, Natty. Let's go.

Natty (*to* **Boy**)   What does that mean? What kind of a question is that to ask a total stranger?

Boy   You're a faggot. Right? I know you are.

Natty   Listen. You've got it . . . all wrong.

Jimmy   No he doesn't.

Natty   Be quiet, Jimmy. Let me handle this.

Boy   I asked you for the time. You were rude. I don't like that. I don't like you.

Jimmy (*to* **Boy**)   Leave him alone.

Boy *advances on* **Natty**.

Boy   Awww. Isn't that sweet? Your man's protecting you. I'm touched. I'm fucking nauseous.

Jimmy   Leave my lover alone.

Boy   Well. Hmmmm. And where does that leave us? I come out for some air. Want to see myself a little scenery. And all around me there are faggots.

Jimmy   Nobody asked you to come here.

Boy   What. Do I need an invitation to walk down the street?

Jimmy   No. Do we?

Boy   Smartass invert.

Natty   Wait. Wait. Let's be reasonable.

Boy   You. You piece of shit. What's reason? You can't reason with sickness. You can't talk man to man or nothing like that. Can you?

Boy *advances on* **Natty**.

Natty   Please don't hurt me.

Boy *advances on* **Natty**. **Boy** *breaks up into hysterical laughter.*

Boy   Oh man. Oh SHIT. I really had you going there, didn't I?

Natty   I . . . I . . .

Boy   HA-HA. You should have seen your face. What a scream.

Jimmy   What the fuck are you doing?

Boy   Go on. Get outta here. Have a nice night.

Natty   You scared me. How dare you scare me.

Jimmy   We're out of here, Natty. Leave this moron alone. You know, you're real pretty. An asshole. But pretty.

Boy   You think I'm pretty? Do you?

Natty   How dare you frighten me. You ought to be ashamed of yourself.

Boy   But I'm not. Fuckface. Fuckface faggot.

Boy *pulls out a knife. It's a casual gesture, as if he's lighting a cigarette.*

Natty   Oh God. Please. I'm . . . I'm not a faggot. I'm not. Don't hurt me.

Jimmy (*comes very close to* **Boy**)   You're such an asshole, Natty. (*To* **Boy**.) Get out of here. GET THE FUCK OUT OF HERE BEFORE I TAKE MY FAGGOT FISTS AND RAM THEM DOWN YOUR THROAT, PUNK.

Boy *stabs* **Jimmy** *repeatedly.* **Natty** *runs away.*

Boy   WHO'S PRETTY NOW. WHO? WHO?

Boy *continues to stab* **Jimmy**. *Lights down on them. Lights up on* **Tilly** *and* **Jaye**. **Tilly** *applies polish to* **Jaye***'s toe-nails. A radio report is heard.*

Radio   Current Central Park temperature is a staggering one hundred and twenty with no drop-off in sight.

Temperature expected to climb to one hundred and forty by daybreak.

Tilly   It's gotten hotter every night since that night.

Jaye   What night?

Tilly   Don't play dumb with me. You get laid and you lose your memory? You know. That night.

Jaye   I told you. I'm not talking about that any more.

Tilly   One day it's sixty degrees. The next day it's a hundred. Weather doesn't happen that way. Look. It's so hot the polish won't dry. It cracks. Like tiny faultlines.

Jaye   It's cheap polish, Tilly. What do you expect from something I lifted off the discount rack at Leroy Pharmacy?

Tilly   You stole this.

Jaye   Uh-huh. On an impulse.

Tilly   Slut.

Jaye   You're a fine one to talk. I saw you stealing fruit at the grocers. Apples. Oranges.

Tilly   I tried to steal bananas but I couldn't fit them in my bra.

Jaye   I don't know if I approve of this.

Tilly   Listen. I stole useful items. I stole food. You indulged yourself. The theft of cheap red nail polish is not exactly defensible.

Jaye   So. Turn me in. I don't care. I hear there's lots of sex in prison.

Tilly   You never let up, do you?

Jaye   Nope. Get used to it.

Tilly   I used to have standards.

Jaye   And then you met me.

Tilly   Jaye. We're middle class. We don't steal.

Jaye   We're impulse thieves. It's probably an illness. Like compulsive shopping. Except we don't pay. And we can't afford to pay, anyway. We spend all our pennies to make rent on an unglamorous shitbox in a menacing neighbourhood. It's an illness. Trust me. God. I love it when you're on your knees.

Tilly   I'm kind of dizzy. Is it possible to get heat-stroke at night?

Jaye   Silly bitch. Do my nails. Go on.

Tilly   I'm thirsty. And cranky. Jaye. Are we unhappy? Are we so unhappy that we steal to fill a void? My God. There are so many things I'd like to take. I'd like to run through the city with enormous shopping carts and fill them with everything.

Jaye   I'd like to fill my shopping cart with multiples of your tongue. And maybe your hands. That way, I wouldn't have to hear you go on and on about this stuff.

Tilly   Take me someplace.

Jaye   You're already someplace.

Tilly   I was thinking . . . a beer run would be nice right about now.

Jaye   Okay. We'll drag out the carts and go shopping. Wake everybody up. Get wild.

Tilly   But then I think, well, I really can't bear to walk past him. He's diminishing. Daily. I don't know whether to laugh or cry.

Jaye   Why not both. If you hit the extremes, you'll eventually get to the middle.

Tilly   You know what. We witnessed a horrible crime.

Jaye   I really can't wait to get back to work. The office is air-conditioned.

Tilly   We witnessed a horrible crime and we've responded by becoming criminals ourselves. We never talk to him. Why not?

Radio static is heard.

Radio   The latest reading from Central Park is a hundred and thirty degrees. An astonishingly rapid increase in temperature has been noted over the last half hour. The Mayor has ordered that all businesses operating within the five boroughs close until further notice. It's . . . VACATION TIME.

Jaye   It's time to make that beer run.

Lights down on **Tilly** *and* **Jaye**. *Lights up on* **Marcel**, *on the job. Every few seconds, we see headlight beams come and go. Lights up on* **Natty**. *He sits at the vanity. As he speaks, he touches the postcards taped to the mirror, one by one.*

Marcel (*to the passing cars*)   Marcel says: Stop. Come directly to jail. Do not pass go. Marcel collects two hundred dollars.

Natty   Morocco has much to recommend it. Sand, for one thing. And intrigue, for another. And of course, there are the boys.

Marcel   Slow down. What's your hurry? Marcel can provide motion in the comfort of your imitation leather interior. All you need's a decent car stereo and a wad of cash to make Marcel a happy camper.

Natty   And Paris, well. It's natural that I would be attracted to the city of light. I love places where I can't understand one damned word spoken. Life's a breeze then.

Marcel   So much traffic and so little time. Boys. BOYS. Take a breather. It's hot and Marcel is sooooo cold. Marcel has a brilliant theory which Marcel will reveal in due course.

Natty   Amsterdam. Now *that's* a city. The prince of cities. I could get lost there. I could. Lost among the blondes. Blondes love me. They don't take me for a coward.

Marcel   Marcel's radiant theory is this: it's so hot that people are keeping to their cars. They mindlessly travel the same stretch of the West Side highway for hours so they can be in the only air-conditioning that still works. But oh, all my children, let me tell *you* what will happen when those cars fizzle out.

Natty   I'm sure I was braver in another life. I just don't know which one. London. I stayed indoors and avoided the food. Jimmy had a splendid holiday while I watched the World Scrabble Championships. I've got to take Jimmy's ashes to Westminster Abbey and hide them under the coronation chair. I mean, who will care?

Marcel   Oh my honey pants, all of you. Your cars will self-destruct on this particular stretch of the gloomy highway. In the sweltering heat you will stagger from the intensity of moiself. And Marcel will wait for you. With a pitcher of ice water and clean pantyhose. Marcel prepares for your coming catastrophe.

Headlights beam directly at **Marcel**. *He's ablaze in light.*

Marcel   THAT'S RIGHT, HON. COME CLOSER. CONSUME ME.

Headlights disappear.

Marcel   Shitshitshit. Marcel's gonna collapse from boredom. Marcel's gonna starve and faint from lack of nourishment. (*Turning his attention to* **Natty**.) Excuse me, Charles Atlas.

Natty   Brave. Braver. Bravest. Seattle. Salt Lake City. Cincinnati.

Marcel   Marcel said: PARDON MOI MR FUCKING UNIVERSE. Marcel would like some food. Marcel would like *you* to provide hors d'oeuvres.

Natty   You broke my music. You scream at me. And you want me to *feed* you?

Marcel   You've invaded Marcel's space. And now you must PAY UP. Food. Glorious food. That is Marcel's desire.

Natty   I have clothes. I can give you a hat. Or a necktie.

Marcel   Marcel says: you are a silly queen. Marcel says: my splendiferous wardrobe is quite complete. AND WHO NEEDS CLOTHES IN THIS AWFUL HEAT.

Natty   Courage is a state of mind. A state. Connecticut. California. Calgary.

Marcel   You are depriving Marcel of a livelihood. Potential clients take one look at the skinny buttless wonder of you and they FLEE. Marcel holds you personally responsible. Marcel finds it a DISGUSTING PERVERSION when moneyed queer boys take to the streets. GET OUT. YOU ARE ECLIPSING THE SUN THAT SPELLS M-A-R-C-E-L.

Natty   I haven't eaten for weeks. I think.

Marcel   Marcel commands you to return to your hovel and whip up some . . . RATATOUILLE.

Natty   Why doesn't Marcel go *home* and cook up some . . . RATATOUILLE?

Marcel   *Nature* is Marcel's home. *Nature* nourishes Marcel. When it rains, Marcel's slender neck drifts elegantly back, Marcel's perfect lips part, and the *rain* feeds Marcel. And sometimes Marcel is nourished by unsuspecting gay boys who stay too long on Marcel's nature preserve.

Natty   I must unpack Jimmy's clothing. I must make contributions to charity.

Marcel   Charity begins at home. Charity begins at night. Charity begins with Marcel. Nourish Marcel. NOW.

Natty   Jimmy always said you were sad.

Marcel   Marcel has serviced the needs of . . . of . . . Neanderthal, Cro-Magnon and Renaissance man. Marcel does not recall a Jimmy man.

Natty   Marcel watched him die.

Headlight beams swing by. A constant stream of light that suggests a mass exodus.

Marcel   Take a break oh all my weary travellers. The night sky burns your eyes, but Marcel has a magic balm. Marcel is but a reflection of the company he keeps. Stop. STOP. TWO ROADS DIVERGED ON A HIGHWAY AND I

COMMAND YOU TO TAKE THE ONE THAT LEADS
TO ME.

Headlights disappear. **Marcel** *returns to his ceramic basin. Takes many pantyhose from his purse and washes them carefully. He lays them out in the street to dry.*

Natty A thousand years ago, when I was a boy and still had hair, I lived above a club on the highway called Ten West. At the time, I was a pharmacist's assistant. I wore white smocks to convince myself I was a professional. At night, I locked myself into my studio apartment and fantasised to the thumping and throbbing music that vibrated beneath my feet. One night, I stood before a mirror and combed my hair for three hours. Beneath me, Donna Summer and Sylvester wailed on. That night, I unlocked my door and entered paradise. I drank a vodka tonic and cried at the bar. Nobody talked to me. I figured it was because in my haste to leave locked doors behind me, I forgot to remove my pharmacist assistant's white smock. On my ninth vodka tonic, I met Jimmy. He tapped me on my shoulder and asked if I was a doctor. I said, no. I'm Natty. He said, so you are. So you are.

Music in: 'Johnny Come Home' (Fine Young Cannibals).

Headlights beam directly at **Marcel**.

Marcel A PENNY FOR YOUR THOUGHTS, SWEET THING.

Headlights disappear.

Natty Natty says: Marcel can use Natty's clothing rack. For the pantyhose. So they dry.

Marcel You wearing that ugly beret because you're bald?

Natty No. No. I have some hair. Some.

Marcel Marcel's tits are melting from the heat and you've got this . . . woollen monstrosity . . . perched on your head. You're sick.

Natty I'm modest.

Marcel   Then do us a favour and cover that mass of undernourishment you call a body. Marcel is not comfortable around starvation.

Natty   I shaved off all my body hair.

Marcel   How nice for you. Marcel knows all about that kind of thing so please spare Marcel the details.

Natty   I'm swimming to England. I've got to bring Jimmy's ashes to Westminster Abbey.

Marcel   Marcel believes we are living in the age of supersonic transport. So you ought to grow back your leg hair and FLY.

Natty   I'm not afraid of flying. But I fear water. So I must . . . swim. Brave. Braver. Bravest.

Marcel   Marcel thought you were harmless. Marcel thought your major problem was that you smelled like an almond. But Marcel is no longer so sure. And . . . WHERE IS THAT DIZZY FAGGOT MUSIC COMING FROM?

Natty   It's the lesbians above the poultry market. They like to dance.

Marcel   There are DYKES in this neighbourhood?

Natty   Uh-huh. They're very cute. Serious types. I think they drink a lot.

Marcel   Well. Marcel says: this is BOYS' TOWN, honey. Marcel says: this is not the neighbourhood for LADIES' HOUR.

Natty   You've never seen them? Dragging groceries and laundry behind them? They do an awful lot of laundry.

Marcel   No fucking way. Marcel converses with MEN.

Natty   Marcel never talked to me. Marcel never talked to Jimmy.

Marcel   Listen here, Mister Sandman. Marcel can spot those who are worth conversing with. Marcel knows a dud

when Marcel spots one. LISTEN UP MY LEZZIE
SISTERS: CUT THE FUCKING MUSIC. DANCE TO
YOUR OWN DIFFERENT FUCKING DRUMMER BUT
LEAVE MARCEL OUT OF IT.

Music gets louder.

Marcel   Marcel speaks and the whole world DOESN'T
LISTEN. Marcel regrets that Marcel was forced to converse
with unseen womanhood. But that is the way the cookie
crumbles here in the meat market.

Natty   You never talked to me. You never talked to Jimmy
while he was bleeding to death in your own backyard.

Music out.

Marcel   Sigh. Oh my ridiculous shrinking boy child. SIGH.
Marcel sighs a big sigh as Marcel recalls the flight of this
pathetic boy child one night not too long ago when there was
blood on the cobblestones and on his chicken-little hands.
Marcel saw all. Marcel speaks THE TRUTH. What were
you doing, sweat pea? Where were *you* running to? Marcel
says: end of fairy tale.

Natty   Courage. Courage in the face of adversity. Danger.
Grab the danger by its horns and ride it. Ride it. I don't. I
don't. I don't wanna die. I am. I am. I am . . . dangerous. I
am dangerous and I am . . . NATTY. I AM NATTY. So
you are, he said. So you are. He swept me off my earthbound
feet and it was many years later I betrayed him.

Music in: 'You Make Me Feel (Mighty Real)', (Sylvester). **Jimmy**
*enters. He dances as if he's dancing in a crowd, all smiles and sweat.
He's doing poppers.* **Marcel** *is awe-struck by this apparent
apparition.*

Natty   Then as now, I wouldn't dance with him. Old habits
die hard. But he danced for me. There's nothing sexier than
watching somebody dance for you. We were so young and so
happy. His body a dazzling intricacy of muscle and
smoothness. His hands yet unblemished by stress, work,

heartbreak. Jimmy. Your body was a testament to youth and so was mine in its half-assed way. The importance we attach to our bodies. They are ephemeral. We are ephemeral and if I could have danced with you that night I would have told you so. Bodies are unimportant until we lose them.

Jimmy   Natty Weldon. Watch me dance for you.

Natty   I'm watching, Jimmy. I'm always watching.

Jimmy   Let's grow up and become Senators. Diplomats.

Natty *approaches* **Jimmy**.

Natty   Let's *not* grow up and avoid the mess.

Jimmy   I like mess. The stuff of life. I'm a dancing fool.

Jimmy *continues to dance.* **Natty** *is motionless, close to him.*

Natty   Beautiful people are allowed to be fools. They can even dance. But the less beautiful are left running after departing trains. Missed connections. You're beautiful, Jimmy.

Jimmy   Someday my prince will come and his name will be Nathaniel. Someday we'll be seventy-five and rail at the indecency of the younger generation. At the old gay home, poppers will be fed to us intravenously and Bette Midler will do the New Year's Eve show.

Natty   How old are you, Jimmy?

Jimmy   I'm twenty years old and I am HOT. Come on. Let me take you on a fast train to meet my folks.

Natty   I'm a coward.

Jimmy   This is the seventies. There's no room for cowardice.

Natty   I was never twenty years old. I'm tired. Jimmy. What if I told you that in fifteen years I will betray you. What if I told you that I will run from you when it counts most. What if I told you that in fifteen years I will watch you die. What then?

Jimmy *takes* **Natty** *into his arms.*

Jimmy There's always the hope that you won't run. The next time.

Natty There's never a next time, Jimmy.

Jimmy Everywhere you look there's a next time.

Boy *enters. Music out.*

Boy Are you a faggot?

Jimmy (*to* **Natty**) Tell me what you'll do. Next time.

Natty I . . . I . . .

Boy You. YOU. Ugly man. Jerkoff. Fuckface. I smell the fear on you. HATE YOURSELF FOR ME. Show me you know what I mean. WHO ARE YOU, BOY?

Natty I'm . . . I'm . . .

Jimmy Hold me close and tell me who you are. Take me places and show me that we will be legion, marching in rows as far as the eye can see and we are all telling each other who we are. Over and over.

Natty I'm . . . I'm . . .

Boy It doesn't matter how I get you. In the end I'll get you all. I'll crush you under my heel because YOU CAN'T TELL ME WHO YOU ARE.

Natty I'm Natty.

Jimmy So you are. So you are.

Jimmy *and* **Natty** *kiss.* **Boy** *pulls out a knife.* **Marcel** *drops to the ground, covering his head with his hands. Lights up on* **Tilly** *and* **Jaye**, *who watch from their apartment.*

Tilly He's got a knife. He's gonna use it.

Jaye Get away from the window.

Marcel   Pleasepleaseplease don't look at me. Don't look at me. Don't look at me.

Boy   You think I'm pretty? How pretty am I? Tell me.

Natty   You ought to be ashamed of yourself.

Boy   But I'm not. I'm taller and prouder and PRETTIER than you.

Tilly   Should we scream or something? I don't know, to chase him away?

Jaye   Get away from the window.

Marcel   I don't wanna be cut. No cuts. No bruises. NO CUTS. Go awaygoawayaway.

Natty   Let's be reasonable. Talk sense.

Jimmy   He's not reasonable, Natty.

Boy   I'm not reasonable.

Natty   You've got a future. It's bright. Put down the knife and talk to us.

Jimmy   He's not reasonable, Natty.

Boy   I'm not reasonable. I'm PRETTY.

Tilly   Let's do something.

Jaye   Why should we?

Marcel   Marcel does not want to see this. Marcel says: NO.

Boy   Faggot. You disgust me. You crowd my world.

Natty   I'm . . . I'm . . .

Jimmy   Hold me close. Hold on.

Boy   GET OUTTA MY NEIGHBOURHOOD.

Natty   I'm . . . I . . . CAN'T.

Boy stabs **Jimmy** *repeatedly.*

Boy   WHO'S PRETTY NOW. WHO? WHO?

Natty *runs away.* **Boy** *runs away.* **Marcel** *rises to look at the carnage.* **Jaye** *joins* **Tilly** *at the window.*

Jaye   Call the police.

Tilly   Okay.

Jaye   It's so . . . quiet.

Tilly   Yeah. We better call the cops.

Jaye   Okay.

A silence, as **Marcel**, **Jaye** *and* **Tilly** *look at* **Jimmy**. *Headlights beam directly at* **Marcel**. *Lights down on all but* **Marcel**.

Marcel   HEY. COME AND SIT WITH ME A WHILE. YOU DON'T EVEN GOT TO PAY. BE WITH ME. BE WITH ME.

Headlights disappear. Light up on **Natty** *at the vanity. Throughout the following scene, he very carefully removes the postcards from the mirror, cuts them up into tiny pieces, and throws them to the wind.*

Natty   We'll never forget, will we, Marcel?

Marcel   What are you talking about silly gay boy? WHAT?

Natty   Where are you from, Marcel? Where is that place that lets you forget?

Marcel   Marcel is a citizen of the universe. Marcel forgets nothing. However, Marcel does employ considerable editing skills. From time to time.

Natty   Sometimes I think I'll be fine in the end. That I'll wake up in the morning and be able to get through the day without telling myself even one lie. But you know, just *thinking* that it's gonna be okay in the end is a lie. So. Where does *that* leave us?

Tilly *and* **Jaye** *enter the street. They drag a shopping cart with them. It's full of beer.*

Marcel   My, my. If it isn't the luscious lushes of Little West 12th Street.

Jaye   Fuck off, freak.

Tilly   Jaye, *really*. (*To* **Marcel**.) Hi. I'm Tilly. This is Jaye. And this is our beer. I think we almost met you at the police station.

Jaye   Yeah. You were looking particularly Jayne Mansfield-esque that morning.

Marcel   Marcel says: lesbians have no manners.

Natty   Hi. I'm Natty. I'm a liar.

Tilly   Oh, great. So are we.

Natty   Really.

Tilly   Sure. We lie all the time. About most everything.

Jaye   We steal, too. We stole this beer.

Marcel   Marcel wants nothing to do with petty thieves.

Jaye   Aren't you an anachronism?

Natty   This is Marcel. Marcel . . . hovers.

Jaye   Why do you refer to yourself in the third person, Marcel?

Marcel   Marcel IS the third person.

Jaye   Heat-stroke. Transvestite clown succumbs to heat-stroke. Melted down in the prime of womanhood. A sad, sad story.

Natty   Did you really steal that beer?

Tilly   Yeah. You ought to see it out there. It's wild. Not a soul in the streets. Supermarkets deserted. Restaurants abandoned. But the cars. Wow. More cars than I've ever seen packed together like . . . like butane lighters waiting to explode.

Jaye   We need the beer 'cause we ain't got air-conditioning.

Natty   I'm trying to be courageous. And everyone's gone. Nobody to watch me spit at passers-by.

Tilly   We're here. You want a beer? I think we almost met you at the police station, too.

Natty   I was the one with the bag over my head, crouching in a corner. If you don't mind, I'll trade you some perfume for a beer.

Jaye   Looks like we're having a block party.

Jaye *removes a small portable radio from the shopping cart.*

Marcel   Marcel must return to work. Marcel has no time for parties.

Jaye   Haven't you heard? They've cancelled work.

Marcel   *Who* cancelled work?

Jaye   The big deals. The men in suits. Though I doubt they're wearing suits at this moment.

Jaye *turns on the* **Radio***. Static. More static. Then:*

Radio   . . . schools, banks, post offices closed. Subway and bus service has been suspended. Current Central Park temperature a hundred and forty-three degrees. A rapid increase in temperature expected by daybreak.

Radio *goes to static.*

Marcel   Marcel, for one, welcomes the heat because the cars will die sooner. Marcel waits with arms spread wide as the widest sea, for all Marcel's children to run back to mama.

Jaye   Uh-huh. Prostitution thrives in hard times.

Tilly (*to* **Natty**) I'm afraid. Really.

Natty   What do you fear?

Tilly   Everything. I'm afraid of cars. Motorboats. Voting.

Marcel (*to* **Jaye**)   Why don't you go live in BROOKLYN with the rest of your sisters? Why don't you leave Marcel to Marcel's business?

Jaye   Looks to me like Marcel hasn't had any business in a long time. Tilly. Look. He's got cobwebs sprouting from his underarms. Lack of use.

Tilly   Mostly, though, I'm afraid I'll lose Jaye. And then I would just crumple up and blow away. Like a picnic napkin. We insult each other a lot, but we like it that way.

Marcel (*to* **Jaye**)   I AM NOT A HE. I AM . . . MARCEL.

Natty   How would you lose her? Why? Well. I guess I'm the last one to be asking those questions.

Tilly   I could lose her the way I met her. In an instant.

Marcel *takes a beer from the shopping cart.*

Marcel   Marcel requires retribution for your insult.

Tilly   I mean, isn't that always true? One minute you know somebody, the next minute you don't. One day you're in love, the next day you're not. You look a girl in the eye and you make a snap judgement. Love makes spontaneous decisions.

Natty   And so does hate. Cowardice.

Marcel   Oh my little ones. Welcome to Marcel's PHILOSOPHY CORNER. Let's see. We've got one horrifically skinny almost naked queer boy and . . . oh my . . . one DRUNKEN DYKE . . . waxing poetic on the nature of our hasty, hasty hearts.

Jaye   Have you got something better to say?

Tilly   I met Jaye at Kennedy Airport. She was to meet a cousin from Los Angeles. I flew into New York looking for a home. I was especially unattractive that day. As I approached the ground transportation exit, I felt a hand grab my arm. I whirled around and it was Jaye. She said –

Jaye   You're ugly, but you must be the one.

Tilly   I couldn't tell if this was a compliment. She took my bags to her car, muttered something about an Uncle Roger.

Jaye   I passed on regards from Aunt Ida.

Tilly   I wondered where we were headed. She said –

Jaye   The barbecue's at three.

Tilly   I mean, who could argue? I began to hallucinate. Maybe I was destined to be in the back seat of a stranger's Honda Civic with no idea of where I was being taken. All I could think about was her eyes. Her funny hat. The way she gripped the steering wheel.

Jaye   I stopped three times so she could vomit.

Tilly   Jesus, was I *sick*. But I couldn't help it. This was completely unlike me, to be in a car with a sexy woman who was wearing a funny hat. A hat with a musical *flower* attached to its brim. Wow. And then, as I was about to pass out from the thrill of it all, she said –

Jaye   I wish I'd known I had such a wacko cousin.

Tilly   I blurted out, but, hey, I'm not your cousin. Stop the car. There's been a mistake.

Jaye   I stopped the car.

Tilly   But there was no mistake. She turned to me. I was a mess. Drool dangling from the corners of my mouth. Acne grew spontaneously, like spores. She said –

Jaye   I know you're not my cousin. I was just testing the quality of your imagination.

Tilly   Oh, sure, I said. But I don't even *know* you.

Jaye   And why the fuck *don't* you know me? Said I.

Tilly   Well. So. Why not? It was true. She looked at me and there was a conspiracy of understanding.

Jaye   Don't believe her. She was squinting a lot. And she adores conspiracy theories.

Tilly   And every year on that day we go back to Kennedy. Sit in tacky bars and make passes at the flight attendants.

Jaye   I *love* flight attendants.

Natty *begins to douse himself with cologne.*

Marcel   Oh nononono. Marcel says: please do not open Doctor Caligari's cabinet again.

Jaye   Why don't you ZIP IT and DRINK UP, Marcel. Or you'll miss the bus to HELL when it rounds the corner.

Tilly   Excuse me. Natty. That's your name, isn't it?

Natty   Jimmy liked airports. We meant to build our vacations around cities that had remarkable airports. But we never managed to get out of New York. There was always something to be done. Always something to do right under your own nose.

Tilly   Look, I didn't mean to make you feel bad. Jaye and me, we're really very fucked up. So don't use us as an example.

Natty   As an example of what?

Tilly   Well. You know. Whatever people use . . . other people . . . as examples of.

Jaye   Natty. Listen. You really shouldn't mix colognes like that. It'll have a bad effect.

Natty   Cologne sustains me. Rivers of cologne. I can't stand my own smell any more. I want to go to meetings. I want to learn how to *like* drugs. I want to visit all the places I've had people mail me postcards from. I want to PARTICIPATE. I WANT HIM BACK.

Natty *clears the vanity with one swipe of a fist. Bottles shatter on the street.*

Marcel   Marcel says: boys will be boys.

Natty   My skin is . . . bubbling. The heat. THE HEAT. LOOK. I'M DEVELOPING BOILS.

Jaye *touches* **Natty** *and jumps back.*

Jaye (*really much more interested in her hand than in* **Natty**) Ouch. Christ. Tilly. We need a towel. And some cold water. This boy's . . . really hot.

Natty (*to* **Jaye**)   I'm gonna burn in hell.

Jaye (*totally uninterested*)   Listen. We're gonna, you know, get some help.

Natty   My limbs are gonna drop off.

Tilly   It's our fault. I knew it. We let that night happen and in doing so, allowed the weather to take over.

Marcel   And why the fuck *shouldn't* the weather take over? I've already seen a ghost tonight. Nothing can compare.

Natty *grabs* **Jaye**.

Natty   You saw it, didn't you.

Jaye   Yes.

Natty   You watched him die.

Jaye (*she pulls away*)   Not . . . exactly.

Tilly   Yes. We did watch him die. The sky split open. The temperature rose. And nothing's been the same since.

Jaye   Well. *That's* true enough. Lately, our lovemaking has come to resemble something out of Genet.

Marcel   Mama said there'd be days like this. There'd be days like this, Marcel's mama said.

Natty   What was it like? Tell me.

Jaye   We called the police. That's what it was like.

Natty   No. I mean. What was it like? To see him die. I didn't. See it. I should have.

Tilly   Don't do this. It's not necessary.

Natty   It is necessary. I've learned practically nothing, it's true. But I do know that. Tell me something. Anything.

Tilly   We watched from above. We thought we were safe.

Jaye   I drank beer and thought . . . how lucky I am not to be him.

Tilly   We called the police. We did. But by that time, there was nothing left to protect us from.

Natty   How could you. How could you . . . *watch?*

Jaye   How could you run?

Tilly   And you know, tell me something. What would you have done? If you were us, if you were a couple of girls holed up in a crappy apartment? Huh?

Natty   I . . . I would have . . . run. Again. And again. I have no pride.

Natty *cries. A silence, as* **Tilly** *and* **Marcel** *busy themselves with anything but* **Natty**. **Jaye**, *forced to take action, pats* **Natty** *half-heartedly on his back.*

Jaye   We saw you a lot, you and your lover. You shopped at all the food stores we couldn't afford. We envied your clothing. We fantasised about what art you'd collect. And each time we saw you we said, we really must invite them up for a drink.

Natty   I was thirty before I told anybody except Jimmy that I was gay. Nobody knew.

Jaye   That's what we all think. Nobody knows. We wear it like it's a medal of honour. We're sick to do it, but we do it anyway. And then one day, we get well. Shake the shame right outta our hair and wonder, well, why in the fuck did we ever let it get the best of us? The trick is to get rid of it. *Before* the point of implosion. Before it eats us to pieces.

Natty   I'm in so many pieces I don't remember what it's like to be whole.

Tilly   And so we said, we really must invite them up for a drink. But we didn't. What did we think would happen?

Headlights beam directly at **Marcel**.

Marcel   And once again, Marcel lifts Marcel's weary shell of a body and entertains the troops. Marcel wears a dress so Marcel can gather all of humankind underneath it. Oh my lonesome dove, are *you* going to help Marcel pass time? Let

me tell you honey, this absolute COW of a dyke called
Marcel an anachronism. What do you think of THAT? Well
At least I am recognizable. AT LEAST I AM THE LAST
OF THE MOHICANS. I saw it, too. DO THEY THINK I
DIDN'T SEE IT? That night, Marcel was collecting
business like it was stardust. Marcel was BUSY. And Marcel
saw the blade strike its target and Marcel hit the street so
fast Marcel didn't notice that Marcel was lying in TRASH.
Animal innards. Guts. COW BLOOD. Marcel sank in
entrails for the better part of an hour before the cops came to
drag Marcel off. Marcel sat in a precinct. Marcel sat in a
straight-back chair whilst no gentlemanly police officer gave
Marcel as much as a HANDY WIPE. Marcel stank. Marcel
was humiliated and covered in debris. But still. Still. Marcel
saw everything and in the end, all Marcel saw was that cool
steel blade. And Marcel realized. MARCEL KNEW THAT
. . . I . . . knew that. I was wearing a dress and some bad
falsies and every ounce of self-preservation kicked in and and
and . . . there was me and my dress and . . . I could cut
myself no slack. I sank. I went way way down that night.
DON'T THEY THINK I KNOW THAT? Oh. My speedy
traveller. Shut off your engine and ignite my transmission.
Teach me to DRIVE. Take it all away. Take me HOME.

*A sudden explosion of blinding hot white light. Just for an instant,
and then it is gone. Radio static is heard.*

Radio   . . . a hundred and sixty-seven degrees and rising.
Unconfirmed reports from Hoboken, Piscataway and Edison,
New Jersey of automobiles spontaneously combusting. And
this just in . . . at Kennedy Airport, a Delta seven-forty-
seven exploded on takeoff. At Port Authority, a Greyhound
bus bound for Lincoln, Nebraska melted within seconds of
entering the Holland Tunnel. Current Central Park
temperature a hundred and sixty-seven and RISING.

Radio *goes to static. A brief silence. Lights down on all but*
Marcel.

Marcel   Marcel Hughes. H-U-G-H-E-S. Yes. That is my
. . . actual . . . name. I was born at 227–27 Horace Harding

Expressway in Queens, New York. My mother, Sally
Hughes, was a practical nurse. Or practically a nurse. I can
never remember which. My father, whose name I cannot
bring myself to utter, was a small businessman. Very small.
He owned a shed, took it to a corner, and called it a news-
stand.

Lights up on **Jaye**.

Jaye   My lover and I were watching television. Yeah.
That's right. She's my lover. You got a problem with that?
Okay. So we're watching television and we hear this noise
from the street. I hear somebody say: FAGGOT. I always
hear that word when it's said. Always.

Lights up on **Tilly**.

Tilly   Jaye and I were watching television. Well, Jaye was
watching. I was looking out the windows, as usual. Excuse
me? No. I do not SPY on people in the street. Well. Actually,
I do. But. Anyway. Jaye was watching a basketball game
and cursing herself because, you know, it was such a dykey
thing to be watching.

Marcel   It was very dark. And I was observing this from
quite some distance. Pardon moi? Oh. I was . . . walking. I
was taking a walk. I often take walks in the neighbourhood.
What? Yes. I LIKE to walk. So, I can tell you that he was
definitely Hispanic. Or a light-skinned black. Pretty skin.
Smooth. Gorgeous. A big guy. Don't you just LOVE big
men?

Jaye   I saw this guy stabbing this other guy. The guy with
the knife was a fair-haired tall white guy. Maybe six foot
three. Broad shoulders. Strawberry blond with freckles.
Good-looking. Like the kind of jerk I used to date before I
got wise. I remember thinking I hadn't seen hair that colour
for a long time.

Tilly   He must have been, oh I don't know, nineteen or
twenty. Small. Delicate. Wiry. With devastating hands. I
adore hands. And this kid had glorious hands. And he

worked out. Great body. Little rippling muscles all over him.
But those hands. Hmmm. Wondrous.

Marcel   Oh yeah. He was a FAT motherfucker. And old.
That sucker was OLD. Forty-five at least. But I think jolly
old fat men are sexy.

Jaye   Other than that, he was pretty nondescript. *You* know
the type. Played some college football. Has a beer gut, but
otherwise, you know, he's in pretty decent shape. He was
attractive, and I couldn't understand how somebody who
was kind of attractive could do such a shitty thing.

Tilly   I can't tell you much about his face, but if you
showed me his hands I'd know. You see somebody use his
hands to kill and you don't forget it.

Lights up on **Natty**.

Natty   Do you know what I recall most vividly? That
Jimmy called me an asshole. Those were his final words to
me, I think. I think . . . why did we survive AIDS, Jimmy
and me, to come to *this*? There's no dignity left. I'd like to go
home now if I may. I can't tell you what he looked like. I
barely saw him. I've got a lot to bury.

Boy *enters. He stands before the group first in profile, then full face.
Then he holds out his hands to them. The group, in unison, with the
exception of* **Natty**, *point fingers at* **Boy**. **Natty** *bows his head,
unable to look.*

All except Natty   That's him.

Lights down on all but **Boy**.

Boy   Makes no difference to me *who* I kill. I could tell you
that it was a *personal* thing. I could tell you about how
goddamned pretty the blade is at night. Out in the open air.
But I'm not *going* to talk about *those* things. I'm gonna let you
put me on the news and I'm gonna nod my head at a lot of
stupid people talking about misunderstanding and
compassion and bad upbringings and I'm gonna fucking
laugh out loud. What? Who said something about bias
crimes? What the fuck is BIAS? This is about HATE. And

there isn't a lawyer or a doctor or any fucked up fucking do-gooder alive who can do a damned thing about it. You wanna fight me, you got to FIGHT me. Lock me up. Come on. Do it. You can take away my blade, but I'm still out there. There's more of me back where I come from.

Lights down on **Boy**. *Lights up on the rest of the scene.*

Empty beer bottles and cans scattered everywhere. **Natty** *has taken to cutting* **Marcel**'s *pantyhose into tiny pieces.* **Marcel** *sits in the shopping cart. He drinks beer.* **Jaye** *spins him around in circles.* **Tilly** *sits among the remnants of the broken cologne bottles. She takes shards of glass and dabs them to her wrists, her neck, any pulse point she can find.*

Tilly   I've never smelled a Chanel perfume before. Hmmmm. It's not as . . . old smelling . . . as I imagined.

Natty   That's Number 19. An elusive scent. Not everyone can wear it.

Tilly   Yeah, well. It suits the s ree .   *a s a s ar o g ass against her wrist.)* Shit. It cut me.

Marcel   Oooooooweeeee. Marcel is a dizzy miss lizzie. Stop the world honey, 'cause Marcel wants to get OFF.

Jaye   We're creating a breeze, Marcel. If we spin long and hard enough, we'll make a typhoon that will carry us to . . . who knows where.

Marcel   Take me to the river.

Jaye (*stopping the cart*)   River's dried up. We could *walk* across to Jersey.

Tilly   Jaye. The Chanel CUT me. I dabbed it on and it fucking CUT me.

Marcel   Don't you bother about that my little Sapphist. Chanel is not an equal opportunity parfumière. Chanel knows which wrists it belongs on.

Tilly   Oh God WHY did we choose to live in a neighbourhood full of gay men?

Jaye   Because we think we *are* gay men.

Tilly Don't start in on me again, Jaye. We're snobs. That's why. We don't even have enough money to buy brand-name toilet paper and we think it's more refined to live with faggots. I swear. I feel like Eliza Doolittle in drag. AND THERE'S NO MORE BEER. WE DRANK TWENTY-SEVEN CASES AND WE'RE NOT DRUNK.

Jaye Look. There are no lights on in Jersey.

Radio static, very loud. Then:

Radio . . . supports have collapsed. Repeat: the George Washington, Triborough, Brooklyn, Manhattan, Williamsburgh and Queensboro bridges have collapsed. Current Central Park temperature one hundred and eighty degrees. Repeat one hundred and eighty and rising.

Marcel Good. So much for the bridge and tunnel crowd.

Natty The neighbourhood is ours again. You'd think I'd be happy about that. But I'm not.

Tilly I'm bleeding. It doesn't hurt, though. You always think you have time. You know, to do certain things. Say whatever needs to be said.

Jaye You do say whatever needs to be said. You talk in your sleep.

Tilly What do I say?

Jaye You talk about . . . Melanie Griffith. Flight attendants. Tarts.

Tilly I've barely gotten used to the way you sleep. And now it's gotten so hot we *can't* sleep. Shit. I can never adjust to change.

Natty *collapses.*

Marcel Girls. GIRLS. EMERGENCY.

Marcel *tries to push himself towards* **Natty**, *who sits bolt upright and speaks with great urgency.*

Natty   Things I ought to have done but didn't: buy a
Jaguar adopt a puppy become an Episcopalian take
communion and I should have been promiscuous when
prosmiscuity was good should have called my dad before he
croaked should have gone to law school should have loved
him truer cleaner braver should have. Could have. Didn't.
BE HANDSOMER LOSE WEIGHT SPEAK MY MIND
FIGHT FIGHT FIGHT BACK.

Marcel   Marcel says: GET ME OUT OF THIS
FUCKING CART.

Tilly *helps* **Marcel** *out of the shopping cart.* **Jaye** *touches* **Natty**,
tentatively, as if she's touching a bug.

Jaye   *He's* awfully hot.

Natty   This is the way it happens. With strangers. One
minute you know somebody. The next minute you're dead.

Sudden explosion of hot white light. Silence. **Marcel** *and* **Tilly** *hold
each other. Headlights beam directly at* **Marcel**.

Marcel   That's the biggest motherfucking car I've ever seen.

Tilly   It's shimmering.

Marcel   Oh my deep-pocketed traveller. Tell Marcel you
are the richest man in the UNIVERSE. Oh my road warrior,
the world is burning up and Marcel doesn't want to miss the
FIRE.

Tilly   It's glowing. Jaye. That car is GLOWING.

Marcel   GLOW MY WAY OH DANNY BOY. BURN
WITH ME.

A car horn is heard. Silence. The horn sounds again.

Tilly   They're honking for you.

Marcel   I'm not going.

Tilly   Why not?

Marcel   I played Mystery Date in high shool. I know the bum's waiting for me behind the door. I KNOW IT.

Natty (*to* **Jaye**)   Tell me why I ran away. Tell me why I'm still running.

Jaye   There's no end to it. Never has been.

Natty   I'm feverish.

Jaye   Uh-huh.

Natty   I like that. Feels like something's . . . happening.

Tilly   Look Marcel. You've got a fucking CUSTOMER. When's the last time one of those rolled through?

Marcel   Marcel is very particular.

Tilly   Who do you think's gonna drive by? There aren't exactly limitless options at this point.

Marcel   I didn't think I'd live to see the day when a lesbian became my pimp.

Tilly   Times change.

Car horn sounds.

Natty   Is there . . . something happening?

Jaye   The city's falling apart. Nothing new there.

Natty   Something's ending. Something's busting up.

Jaye   Yeah. I feel that way every time I take the subway.

Car horn sounds.

Marcel (*considering this carefully*)   I like to travel. I like to FLY.

Tilly   Wow. That car is . . . LEVITATING.

Marcel   Oh mymymy. WAIT FOR ME, PETER PAN. Marcel's going to places where there is no slime to sink down into. Where the big girl's shop is always OPEN.

Marcel *tidies himself up, starts towards the headlights. An explosion of hot white light, and he's gone.*

Radio   . . . no longer registering. Temperature can no longer be measured. Two hundred degrees at last reading. Last reading. Last reading. Barometric pressure is at a standstill. Jones Beach has fallen into the Atlantic. We advise all residents to –

Radio *goes to static.*

Tilly *gathers up a pair of* **Marcel***'s pantyhose and wraps them around her wrist.*

Tilly   I can't stop bleeding.

Natty   This is the way it happens. This way.

Tilly   But it's slow.

Natt   With strangers.

Tilly   And unpredictable. Shit. Now what. I'm turning into a SHRINE. I'll bleed forever and people will kneel at my feet. They'll light candles. Make offerings.

Natty   I'm shivering. Sick. I'm paying for something.

Jaye   Bullshit. We never pay for anything. Be quiet.

Tilly *kneels at the ceramic basin. She submerges her head in it. While* **Natty** *speaks, she bangs her head into the basin. Slowly. Rhythmically.*

Natty (*a great realization*)   Something's busting up. I'm . . . imploding. A fluorescent bulb I am a bulb a light a sickness an arrested development an ember the world in my pocket and and and I WANT HIM BACK I WANT A CHANCE TO NOT DIE IN THIS HEAT I WANT I WANT –

Jaye   Shut up. SHUT UP. MY GIRLFRIEND'S GOT FUCKING STIGMATA. Shut. The fuck. Up.

Music in: 'Intro: Prelude to Love/Could This Be Magic' (Donna Summer). **Tilly** *snaps to attention. Her hair and face are soaked with* *water and bits of blood.* **Tilly** *and* **Natty** *bop along to the music. It fills them with an odd sense of determination and direction.*

Jaye   What the fuck . . .

Tilly   I'm melting. I'm bleeding and wet and God. I LOVE THIS SONG.

Natty   Dress me.

Jaye   It's too hot for clothes. Be quiet. Tilly. TILLY. LOOK AT ME.

Tilly   I can't. I'm too busy falling apart.

Jaye   Why won't you look at me?

Tilly   Don't know. Don't know.

Natty   Clothe me. In white.

Jaye   And where is this music coming from? WHERE?

Tilly   Nineteen seventy-something. Before we were mean.

Natty   Beore we lost time. Please. Dress me up and take me to a DISCO.

Natty *and* **Tilly** *continue to dance.* **Tilly** *removes her blouse.*

Jaye   What are you doing?

Tilly   Melting. Moulting. Something.

Tilly *undresses completely. She rifles through the clothing rack. She finds a dazzling white suit.* **Natty** *begins to shake violently. He falls to his knees.* **Jaye** *cradles him.*

Jaye   I've never held a man in my arms like this. Never wanted to. Still not sure I want to.

Natty   So cold. So . . . fucking . . . cold. We're burning up.

Jaye   Have I always been this mean? Have I? God. If it's true I'll slit my throat.

Tilly *puts on the man's suit jacket. The pants. They are ridiculously large on her. She goes to* **Jaye** *and* **Natty**, *kneels beside them. Her hair, if possible, seems to get wetter.*

Jaye (*touching* **Tilly**'s *face*)   Baby. You look . . . deranged. You're so wet.

Tilly   Hey. You never touch me in public.

Jaye   Things change.

Natty *continues to shiver, but he's happy, he's smiling. The music is loud and glorious.* **Jaye** *kisses* **Tilly**.

Tilly   Wow. You kissed me. And I'm not even drunk.

Natty   Take me to a disco and play this song over and over. Make it sweet. Make it pretty. Make it count. Help me. Clothe me. CLOTHE ME.

Tilly *and* **Jaye** *dress* **Natty** *in* **Tilly**'s *clothing. Her blouse. Her slacks. Whatever. Strangely, they fit him rather well.*

Tilly   Water and blood pouring out of me. I feel so clean. I'm shedding myself.

Jaye   You're glorious. A mess, but glorious.

Natty   My heart is breaking it's busting up I'm fine I'm happy I need . . . contact . . . make contact. MAKE CONTACT. PLEASE. PLEASE. MAKE THEM UNDERSTAND. WE ARE NOT . . . WE ARE NOT COWARDS.

Jaye *removes* **Tilly**'s *jacket. She then removes her own blouse.*

Natty   I can't stand all this. Beauty. I can't.

Jaye *grasps* **Natty**'s *hand, tight. She bends to take* **Tilly**'s *breast into her mouth.*

Tilly   Oh God. We're so close to the edge, we can't even see it coming.

Jaye *and* **Tilly** *begin to make love. The music continues, insistent.* **Natty** *holds on to* **Jaye**'s *hand.* **Jimmy** *enters. He's dressed in white from head to toe. He holds a knife.*

Natty   Jimmy. Oh Jimmy where have you gone. Where are you going to.

Jimmy   I'm on my way. Be on my way with me.

Jimmy *pulls* **Natty** *to his feet.* **Jaye** *and* **Tilly** *continue to make love.*

Natty   Where are we going?

Jimmy   We're going to Ten West. We have a date.

Natty   But I lost my hair. I can't go anywhere.

Jimmy   We're going to make you well. Take this.

Jimmy *gives* **Natty** *the knife.*

Natty   Jimmy. This is a knife. A weapon.

Jimmy   It's a beginning. Tear up the world for me. Make your mark.

Jimmy *leads* **Natty** *to the enormous map of the meat-packing district. He takes* **Natty**'s *hand, lightly tracing over the map with the knife.*

Jimmy   It's easy to get someplace if you know where you're going. Look. Look how we're gliding through.

Natty *slashes through the map with the knife. Again. And again.*

Jimmy   Time to fly, Natty Weldon.

Natty   Lift me.

Jimmy *lifts* **Natty** *into his arms. They step through the map. They're gone.* **Jaye** *and* **Tilly** *are a splendid sight amid the ruin. A glorious flash of white light and they disappear.*

The torn-up map begins to shake, violently.

Blackout.

Disappeared

In memory of Pat, with love and thanks

The Time
One Sunday evening in New York City, and at various times
preceding and following that evening.

The Place
A run-down bar in Hell's Kitchen; a railroad apartment in Hell's
Kitchen; an Upper East Side thrift shop; an Upper East Side
apartment; a midtown police station; a Lower East Side travel
agency.

The Setting
This is a barren landscape with touches of the otherworldly. It
should appear as if everything here, while maintaining certain
aspects of naturalism, appears from nowhere.

Note
The use of capitals in certain passages does not necessarily or
exclusively indicate a rise in speaking volume. However,
capitalization always suggests a shift in intensity or emphasis.
Similarly, the use of 'beats' does not suggest the use of pauses.
Rather, the beats indicate shifts in thought, sometimes quite abrupt
shifts. The punctuation often does not conform to standard
punctuation as sentences are sometimes broken where one might
not expect them to be broken, and often what might naturally be
written as a question is written as a statement. Strict attention
should therefore be paid to the punctuation pattern as it does create
the text's rhythm. Blackouts should not be used at all as the action
from scene to scene should proceed with fluidity. The music
selected for the play is not random. It relates very specifically to the
text; therefore, no substitutions should be made.

Act One

One

Music in: 'Elenore' (The Turtles). **Elston** *and* **Sarah** *at a seedy dive of a bar.* **Jack** *tends bar.* **Elston** *wears an ill-fitting tuxedo. His hair is slicked back. He looks ridiculously out of place. He watches* **Sarah** *dance. She's having a great time dancing by herself.* **Jack** *also watches her dance. Eventually,* **Sarah** *winds her way over to* **Elston**. *She performs for him, lip-synching to the tune. She runs her hands over the lapels of his tux. She's playful and not at all sexually suggestive.* **Elston** *pays her no mind. It's as if she isn't there. Unable to get a response from* **Elston**, **Sarah** *gives up. She sits at the bar and smokes.*

Sarah   They wrote that song about me. Did you know that, Jack?

Jack *shrugs.*

Sarah   I wasn't even born at the time. But it's about me, anyway. The guy who wrote it, he had a dream of the most fantastic woman he'd ever meet and it was me. How I look now. Did anybody ever write a song about you, Jack?

Jack *shrugs.*

Sarah   Yeah. So. This guy, he's a Brit and he breaks out in sweats over his dream and so he writes this song. And his buddies in the band, they say, well bloody great, kid. But what's her name? So he says, dunno. Eleanor. Maybe. Then my mother fucks the whole deal and names me Sarah. Right? So. Ten years ago maybe, I'm listening to the radio and I hear this song and I know it's all about me. And I'm freaking out because, Jesus, I know it's the song I'm born to hear. I write the guy a letter, you know, send him a picture. I write, hey, I'm Eleanor but my name's Sarah and I hope you'll understand. The bastard never wrote back. I heard he was dead. Serves him right. But you know, then it gets really creepy. You know what happened then, Jack?

Jack *shrugs.*

Sarah   I'm at this Springsteen concert, I don't know, five years back, right? And this geezer comes up to me. I mean, this guy's so old his skin is yellow and he wheezes. Got real long hair. Yellow-white. And he grabs me, you know? Strong. For an old bag. And his breath, oh man, it was like . . . dirt. Heavy. Like overwhelming . . . grime. I think he wants to touch me or, I don't know, something. And he leans in real close and whispers, 'Eleanor. How lovely to see you again.' Creepy, right? Well. What do you think of that, Jack?

Jack *shrugs.*

Sarah   I'm thinking maybe I should write it up for a magazine.

Elston   Jack be nimble. Jack be quick.

Jack *and* **Sarah** *consider this.*

Jack   You wanna drink, mister?

Elston (*to* **Sarah**)   Jack be nimble. Jack be quick. It's from a song. 'The Limbo Rock'.

Sarah   Uh-huh. Yeah. So?

Elston   A lyric. (*He sings.*) Jack be nimble, Jack be quick. Jack jump . . . I don't remember the rest of it exactly. But it's a song. About Jack. It's fate.

Sarah   Wait. Are you saying that somebody wrote a song about Jack? And that it's fate?

Elston   No. I'm saying that your meeting with the geezer was fate.

Jack   I've never heard this song you're talking about.

Elston   I'm saying that the geezer was affirming your belief. Fate.

Sarah   Yeah. Well. Maybe he thought I was his long lost granddaughter, too.

Elston It's possible. But not likely. Consider the statistics. In a group of one hundred women, what are the odds that even one of them will be called Eleanor?

Sarah I don't really know. What do you think, Jack?

Jack Dunno. Unless you was sitting in a room full of Roosevelts, I'd have to say the odds would be pretty low.

Elston Exactly.

Sarah Course, maybe there was a run on the name after the song came out. There's lots of Eleanors. Eleanor Parker. Eleanor Rigby.

Jack Eleanor Connolly. (*Beat.*) My ex.

Elston Jack, if I am remembering correctly, and I am not at all sure that I am, Chubby Checker sang 'The Limbo Rock'.

Sarah So what are you saying? Some old creep with bad breath calls me Eleanor and this means there's UFOs hiding out in a barn in Nebraska?

Elston I'm saying you believe. In fate. In the notion that nothing is random.

Sarah Right. And we're getting looped in some shit-hole on the West Side Highway 'cause we knew we were gonna do it and so that's why we're here.

Elston You believe the song was written about you. Fact?

Sarah Yeah. It was.

Elston And you said that your meeting with the geezer was . . . creepy? Is that what you called it?

Sarah Yeah. Creepy. Like you.

Elston In my book, Sarah, creepiness is a synonym for what we are afraid to recognize as our own. The very things we ought to embrace but will not. Embrace it. Sarah.

Sarah Uh-huh. Well. What do you think this guy does, Jack?

Jack Dunno. Suit don't fit him.

Sarah   Yeah. Like he got lost on his way to a New Year's Eve party a billion years ago. You a fan of *The Twilight Zone*, Jack?

Jack   Oh sure. Love the one where that kid wishes everybody into a cornfield. I like that.

Sarah   Oh God I wish I could do that. Wish people into cornfields. My boyfriend. My mother. This . . . creepy . . . guy.

Elston   Don't you like my clothing? I wore it for you.

Sarah   You hear that, Jack? This fuck wore a monkey-suit for me.

Elston   I usually don't talk this much. You must be special.

Sarah   Your technique's a little creaky. Try again.

Jack   Mister. You wanna buy Sarah a drink?

Elston   No. She drinks too much. I've noticed.

Jack   You wanna buy me a drink? 'Cause if you don't buy somebody a drink I'm gonna have to ask you to leave.

Elston   I'm sorry. I mean no disrespect. I'll drink whatever you give me. Please.

Jack   You wanna beer?

Elston   Whatever you'd like.

Jack   Jack Daniels?

Elston   It doesn't matter.

Jack   Come on, guy. What? Whiskey sour? Gin tonic? Decide.

Elston   I trust you, Jack.

Jack   Oh fuck me. I get one customer and he's a wacko faggot.

Elston   There's no need to get touchy, Jack.

Sarah   Don't mind Jack. He calls everybody a faggot. It's a term of endearment. Some kinda Irish thing. I know. My mother's the same way.

Elston   Are you Irish, Sarah?

Sarah   Yeah. What are you?

Elston   I'm an entertainment attorney.

Jack   Look. I don't care what you are. Just order.

Elston   All right. A Stoly Martini. Olives.

Sarah   A real lawyer drink. A real . . . creepy . . . lawyer drink.

Elston   Why do you say that, Sarah?

Sarah   What's an entertainment attorney doing in a dive?

Elston   A little bird told me you'd be here.

Sarah   You're so full of shit it's coming through your shoes. What are you really? Pimp? Truck driver? Atomic scientist?

Elston   I'm an entertainment attorney. Got lots of clients. You ever been to Ireland, Sarah?

Sarah   Who are your clients? Name them.

Elston   Ireland is beautiful, Sarah. I've been there fifteen times. On business.

Sarah   Your client list. Give it to me.

Elston   Business takes a man places. Do you know what it's like to be in business, Sarah? Do you know what it's like to travel? (*Beat.*) I have many clients. The Turtles. For instance.

Sarah   You're lying.

Elston (*he sings*)   Eleanor, gee I think you're swell . . . coincidence? Or fate?

Jack   You manage turtles?

Sarah   Shut up, Jack. (*To* **Elston**.) Go on. I'm listening.

Elston   There's nothing more to say. I'll finish my drink and be gone. If you'd like, I'll send you a couple of tickets to their next concert.

Sarah   Nah. I'm kinda busy. And I have a fear of flying. But thanks, you know, for asking.

Elston   I'll leave you my card. If you change your mind.

Elston *gives* **Sarah** *a business card.*

Sarah   Timothy J. Creighton. Entertainment attorney. Yeah. Sure.

Elston   You shouldn't doubt me, Sarah. Sarah Casey.

Sarah   How'd you know that?

Elston   Coincidence. Or fate.

Sarah   Yeah. Well. That's not my name. So much for conspiracy theories.

Jack   Who said something about conspiracies?

Sarah   SHUT UP, JACK. (*To* **Elston**.) All right. Out with it. What do you want?

Elston   They call this Hell's Kitchen.

Sarah   Great. A tourist.

Elston   No. I . . . I live on the East Side. I was walking. I like to walk. At night. I like the river. I was thirsty. I stopped.

Sarah   You like to drink.

Elston   I like to drink.

Sarah   And you don't really like to talk. But you talk to me because I'm special.

Elston   Yes. And you have kind eyes.

Sarah   And I bet you think I have a big heart, right?

Elston   Yes.

Sarah A big-hearted hooker. Is that what you think? Guess what. I'm not. Do you understand that? Do you think he understands that, Jack?

Jack *shrugs.*

Elston I don't think you're a hooker. I think you're kind.

Sarah This is where I live, okay? I have a job. You think there's nobody decent living on this side of town? Is that it? Because you are wrong. I'm not some lonely piece of ass losing myself in a booze-bag joint. I'm not.

Elston I'm sorry you're so defensive.

Sarah And I am not impressed by your business card Mr Timothy J. Creighton. Are you, Jack?

Jack Nah. See lots of his type. Skinny. Lip sores.

Sarah Creepy-looking bastard liar who looks as much like a lawyer as I do a brain surgeon.

Elston All right. I'll tell you what I really do. I kill people.

Jack (*after a beat*) No shit. For a living?

Elston No. I just kill.

Jack You don't get paid for it?

Elston No. I do it. That's all.

Jack Sonofabitch. How many people you pop?

Elston Six. Maybe seven.

Jack You're not sure?

Elston I'm not certain that one died. She might have lived.

Jack Yeah? Where you been doing this killing?

Elston Here. Upstate. Different places. I like here best.

Jack Yeah. More of a selection, right?

Elston That's right. And anonymity. It's important.

Jack Sure it is. Where do you do them? In the street? Just like that?

Elston   No. I take them home. And then I do them. In my apartment. I tend to keep them alive a few days. Before.

Jack   Oh. I get it. Like you're fattening them up and stuff. Yeah.

Elston   No. I don't feed them. I talk to them. For a while. Before.

Jack   Okay. And then. Then what? You . . . shoot them?

Elston   I drown them. In my bathtub. They put up terrific struggles. I love to watch them fight. You ever drown anyone, Jack?

Jack   I drowned a mouse once. Took a fuck of a long time.

Elston   Yes. And people take a fuck of a long time, too.

Jack   Uh-huh. And I guess this entertainment lawyer shit, I guess you just made that up.

Elston   No. There is a Timothy J. Creighton and he is an entertainment attorney. Although I'm quite certain he doesn't represent The Turtles.

Jack   So this, uh, suit. It ain't yours?

Elston   No. It's his.

Jack   And you just took it, right?

Elston   I borrowed it. I manage a thrift shop. Many people dropping off many clothes and other . . . belongings. I have regular customers.

Jack   Okay. I get it. You put on some other guy's old gear and then you go out and whack girls. Makes sense.

Elston   Exactly my point, Jack. I am Mr Creighton when I wear his clothing. I am exceedingly wealthy and I live on East Seventy-Fifth Street. My wife is called Rachel and we are fond of making trips to the Cape. But Mr Creighton is compelled to kill people. Coincidence. Or fate?

A tense beat. **Elston** *breaks out into a broad smile.* **Jack** *laughs.*

So. How about another Stoly Martini, Jack. And whatever our friend Sarah would like.

Jack   I gotta hand it to you, mister. You had me going there right at the end. Jeez, that part about the clothes. You know, it's like, it's –

Elston   Creepy?

Jack   Bet your ass. Jeez. Wow. I'm a fucking sucker.

Elston   Fucking faggot sucker.

Jack (*laughs*)   Yeah. Fucking fag sucker. *Salut.*

Sarah   So what's your name. Really.

A beat before **Elston** *answers.*

Elston   Tim. Tim Creighton.

Sarah   Okay. Tim Creighton or whoever you really are. I gotta be up real early tomorrow and I'm so mad at my boyfriend I'm gonna take a hatchet to his face. I'll leave you here with Jack. You can trade stupid jokes and then maybe you can make him your first male victim. As for me, I got to get some sleep. Some of us work day jobs.

Elston   What do you do, Sarah?

Sarah   I'm a linebacker for the Giants. Satisfied?

Elston   No, really. I'm interested in the way you live.

Sarah   I bet you are. How about if I told you I'm a prison guard at Rikers Island? While I'm beating the inmates I have fantasies about replacing Sybil Danning in films like . . . PRISON DAMES IN HEAT. Yeah. Sarah Casey, muscles of steel, stars in BABES BEHIND BARS.

Elston   So your name is Casey. Sarah Casey. I guessed your name. Fate.

Sarah   So what. Some creeps are lucky.

Jack   She works in a travel agency.

Sarah   Shut up, Jack.

Jack   It's her uncle's shop. Down on East Seventh Street. Sells Warsaw package deals to old Polacks.

Sarah   You're disgusting, Jack.

Elston   That must be nice for you, Sarah. Working as a travel agent.

Sarah   Yeah. I'm thrilled.

Elston   Your boyfriend. What's his name?

Sarah   Who knows. I used to go with Jack, here. But then I discovered he was an idiot savant. His talent is pouring beer. He's real good at it. But I figure, see, there's no future in it. Jesus. I gotta get out of this city. I'll be brain-dead, I keep hanging with crap like you two.

Elston   You're a smart girl, Sarah. You'd like to travel. You dream of fame. Fortune. It's out there.

Sarah   Listen, asshole. I can play the tough broad with a minimal amount of brains as well as the next girl. And that's fine. That's just . . . fine. For people like you.

Elston   And why is that fine?

Sarah   It's what you expect. Young tart parks her ass on a barstool on Forty-Eighth and the highway. You think, sure, she's fair game. Nice girl. Not too much upstairs. Has a way with men and hairspray. I play along because there's no investment in you. I tell you nothing. You get . . . nothing. I remain intact. Yes. I work in my uncle's travel agency while I attend night classes at some second-rate city college. Yes. I dream of many things and no, I am not deluded by unreasonable expectations of a future dazzling life.

Elston   And yet you believe that a man who lived several thousand miles away wrote a song about you before you were even born.

Sarah   Yeah. And you drown women in your bathtub. We're a couple of charmers, aren't we?

Elston   You have kindness. You do. Sarah Casey.

Sarah   Thank you. Thanks for the booze, Jack. I'm outta here.

Elston   Do you really think I look ridiculous?

Sarah   (*considers this*)   Absolutely.

Elston   I know I do. I dress this way because it's the only way people pay attention to me. Normally, I recede. Like Jack's hairline.

Sarah   You're a pretty funny guy, Mr Timothy J. Creighton.

Elston   You're the only woman who's talked to me.

Sarah   You're a sad man, right?

Elston   Lonely.

Sarah   Oh. That, too. And I'd guess you collect things. What? What do you collect?

Elston   Stickpins. Gloves. Spectacles. Accessories. The trappings of things. (*Beat.*) And you don't collect anything. You go to the movies.

Sarah   Romantic comedies are my specialty.

Elston   Boy gets girl. Boy loses girl.

Sarah   Boy cries. Those are my favourites.

Elston   And then?

Sarah   And then. One night at a shitty rock concert, a dirty old maniac mistakes the girl for somebody he once fucked in a brothel. He calls her Eleanor. She finds it all very creepy. She goes home and passes out. She gets up the next morning. And the next. And maybe the next. That's all. The end.

Jack   I never saw a movie like that.

Elston   Shut up, Jack.

Jack   Hey. Fuckface. Don't you dare tell me to shut up.

Sarah   Jack was a Golden Gloves champ.

Jack   Fuck me, yes. Light-heavyweight. Won twice. Subnovice and Open classes.

Sarah   He could have been a contender.

Jack   Fuck me, yes. I was a contender.

Sarah   Of course, Jack was going to be a cop. But. It didn't quite work out. He lost his hair, instead. We're old friends.

Jack   Family friends.

Elston   You have a large family, Jack?

Jack   The largest. Yeah.

Elston   I'm an orphan. I was raised in a void.

Sarah   Weren't we all. It's late, boys.

Elston   But it's not too late for you to talk with me. Sit a while.

Sarah   Nope. The early bird gets the worm, et cetera.

Elston   You're an early bird. A kind bird.

Sarah   I'm really not so kind. I'm not.

Elston   I know. That's why I like you. Sit with me. Call me Tim. And I'll call you Eleanor.

Sarah   Why?

Elston   Because you deserve it. (*Beat.*) I'll tell you stories.

Sarah   What kind of stories?

Elston   True stories.

Sarah   And will they be sad stories?

Elston   If you'd like.

Sarah   Do you know any UFO stories?

Jack   There's this UFO that landed in somebody's backyard in Maine. It lands in the backyard and gets caught up in a clothes-line. And all the clothes get caught up, you know, overalls and stuff, 'cause it's the backyard of farmers, so there's lots of denim.

Sarah   This is not a true story, Jack.

Jack   I swear it's true. And these people, these farmers, they come running out and all their clothes are like, electrified. Electric current's running through their overalls and underwear and it's like watching a moving neon beer sign, you know, a blue one? 'Oh Jesus,' says this one farmer, 'we got to do something about this shit.' And while he's scratching his head wondering what he's gonna do, the electricity eases off and this farmer notices that all his clothes have turned white. The UFO's sucked all the colour from his clothes. Then, he hears music. Violins and shit coming from the UFO.

Sarah   Who told you this?

Jack   Wait. So. This little fat guy smoking a cigar comes out of the UFO and he says to the farmer, he says: 'Upon this rock you will build my church.' Then, the fat guy blows smoke at the farmer and disappears. Poof. Just like that. So. The farmer uses the UFO as a church, builds an altar and some pews inside, like, 'cause he goes inside and it's completely empty. No controls. No gears. No nothing. And there it sits until this day. He kept the clothes-line up, the one with all the white clothes, as proof. The farmer's got a cable TV show, too.

Sarah   You're an asshole, Jack.

Jack   It's the truth. State police even found the fat guy's cigar stub. They keep it at the local station-house. Framed in glass. It's evidence.

Elston   We like evidence, don't we, Jack?

Jack   Sure. It's like . . . proof. That stuff happened.

Sarah   Stuff happens all the time to you, Jack. And you couldn't prove it. Stupid fuck. If somebody walked in here and levitated you'd probably claim he was Saint Anthony.

Jack   I'm religious. It ain't natural for men to walk on air.

Sarah   They don't.

Elston   Some men walk on air.

Sarah   Yeah? Tell me about it. Tim. Tell me a story about a man who walks on air.

Elston   I shall. Sit a while. Sit.

Two

Jack's press conference. He speaks to the audience. He squints, as if he's under hot bright lights.

Jack   Okay. You guys ready with the light? Right. So where was we? Oh. Yeah. So there we was, the perp and me. Eyeball to eyeball. Me and the perpetrator of the alleged aforementioned crime. And I told Sarah, I said, look woman: this guy ain't kosher. He's like some weirdo in a waiter's outfit trying to pass himself off as a representative of the legal profession. But she was real big on him. Impressed by his clothes and his business card, which, the perp had told us, was borrowed. I knew right off. I knew this guy was a killer. He told us he was. And I take people at their word. I'm a smart guy. And he wasn't pulling nothing over my eyes. But Sarah, well, she always had a weakness for little men. Not me. Like I said, I knew right off. Let me tell you something. This guy had these like . . . little sprouts of hair growing out of his lip. And you gotta figure that's bad news. You figure, a guy around, what is he? Thirty, forty? And he can't grow facial hair? What is that? That's like . . . bad hormones. It's shit. It's . . . perverted. Also, I gotta tell you about his ears. This friend of mine, he's seen a lot of weird stuff in certain areas of the Northeast Corridor, and he told me about killer ears. I swear, yes, there is such a thing. All killers got the same ears. A German doctor did a study on thirty or forty of them. Guys like Speck, who popped off the nurses in Chicago. And Berkowitz. You know, the wacko who killed at the command of a dog? Oh man, whattya gonna say about a guy who takes orders from a fucking Labrador? So. They got these little tiny ears. No lobes. Like that Nimoy guy from *Star Trek*. Well, they all got ears like that, only less pointy. And this German doctor proved that

all killers have these ears. Look it up. It's evidence. It's all
. . . fucked up. This Creighton character, he had those ears.
I noticed straight off. But I didn't say nothing 'cause, well,
maybe he wasn't. A killer. But was I afraid of him? Nah. Not
me. I warned Sarah. I told her. And now it's her own fault
she's up and disappeared. Women don't listen. Women don't
wait. Sarah and me, we go way back. I'm all broke up, but
whattya gonna do? Life proceeds. I won two Golden Gloves.
Did I tell you that? I won. Twice.

Three

Ellen *at home in Hell's Kitchen, with* **Ted Mitchell**.

Ellen   Or some ice cream. I got that. Wouldja like some
vanilla, officer?

Ted   No, ma'am. I'm here to ask you things.

Ellen   Which things?

Ted   Things. About Sarah.

Ellen   I told you what I know. She didn't say much. Not a
talkative type. Worked downtown in my brother's travel
agency. Talked about getting her own place. Never got
around to it. She was twenty-five. We had our problems. I
can show you pictures of her when she was little.

Ted   Mrs Casey. Did Sarah mention any friends, male
friends? Was she . . . did she have lots of boyfriends.

Ellen   What are you implying? Just what are you saying
about my Sarah?

Ted   Nothing. I want some background is all.

Ellen   Sarah had a fella. Skinny little guinea bastard.
Anthony. I hated him. She did, too. You talk to him? Go
ahead. My Sarah, she had shitty taste but she was faithful.
My daughter was no slut.

Ted   I never implied she was. Your daughter is missing, Mrs Casey, and it is my obligation to uncover every lead, no matter how trivial or unpleasant.

Ellen   She's dead.

Ted   We don't know that.

Ellen   You have kids, officer? You got girls?

Ted   I have sons.

Ellen   You don't worry about boys. Girls, well, they're easier to talk to but you worry. Not that Sarah and me talked. We hardly talked at all. She was moody. She went to night-school. What could I say to her? You think about all these things and you don't say any of them and then your kid dies.

Ted   There is no evidence that your daughter is dead, ma'am. Please. Talk to me. The contents of her room, was there anything missing? A scrap of paper with a telephone number. Anything.

Ellen   There's a single bed with an extra firm mattress and a burnt sienna crocheted blanket which I made for Sarah when she was twelve and a half. She asked for burnt sienna because she thought it was the saddest colour in the whole Crayola box. It looked good on that *Eyewitness News* telecast, didn't it? Are you sure you don't want some ice cream?

Ted   I'm sure. Thank you.

Ellen   Well, that's it. For her room, I mean. Oh yeah. There's a desk with nothing in it. And the record.

Ted   What kind of record?

Ellen   You saw it when you looked around with your friends. The one that's nailed to the wall. She bought it years ago. Wore out the grooves from playing it so much so she broke it in half. Then she felt so guilty about breaking it, she taped the damned thing back together and nailed it to the wall. Over her bed. She actually thought it was alive, that record. Told me some foreigner wrote the song for her. You think that's a nice thing for a mother to hear? She didn't do no drugs, but she was crazy. If they'da had therapy when she was a kid, I woulda sent her.

Ted I have two sons, Mrs Casey. And I do worry about them. I know how you feel. And I'd be alarmed, too, if this had happened to either of them. I'm a parent. I sympathize.

Ellen I'm not alarmed. I'm grieving.

Ted That's . . . perfectly reasonable given the circumstances, but we haven't the facts –

Ellen Facts? I don't give a shit about facts. I know what I know. And I know things. In my gut. Like I know my Sarah is gone. Lost to me and to this fucking life she coulda had. I hear her calling. Calling to me. But it's from someplace far away enough so you can hear but you cannot touch. You know what I feel like? I feel like bowling. Heaving a big ball down an alley and having a bunch of big guys throwing their big balls down the alley next to mine. I wanna make a bunch of noise. Lots of noise so I can drown out the sound of my kid calling out to me.

Ted We're doing what we can.

Ellen You know what she's saying to me? She says, Ma, why'd you have to be such a fucking lousy parent. Over and over. Just that one thing. Well. She wasn't much of a talker. (*Beat.*) Maybe you'll be wanting some of that ice cream now, huh?

Four

Sarah *and* **Elston** *at the travel agency.* **Elston** *wears glasses and sports a moustache.*

Sarah I'm sorry Mister . . .

Elston Jonas. Mister Paul Jonas.

Sarah Yes. Mister Jonas. There really aren't any junkets to Siberia.

Elston I didn't think there would be. But I figured, hey, it's worth a try. It's a hard place to get to. By yourself. I thought maybe a group, maybe there'd be a group of people who shared my curiosity about the place. I'm very curious about Siberia. Aren't you?

Sarah I guess I am. Curious. About different places.

Elston But not about Siberia?

Sarah No. Not really. I'm sorry.

Elston That's okay. You're honest. I like that in a travel agent. So many agents trying to sell you so many packages. So many bad packages. They'll sell you anything for a commission. And with so many people travelling these days. So many Americans travelling.

Sarah Uhm. Yes.

Elston Business must be good for you.

Sarah Fairly good. Yes. So. You've got, let me see if this is right. You've got four weeks and you would like to go –

Elston Someplace cold. And distant.

Sarah Cold and distant. I see.

Elston Well, because of heat-stroke.

Sarah You don't do well in heat. I understand.

Elston Oh, no. No, no, no. It's not me I'm worried about. I'm very healthy. It's others who worry me. I can't bear seeing people succumbing to the effects of heat. I'm queasy. You go someplace cold, you don't have to put up with that sort of thing.

Sarah That's true. Perhaps Europe. It's off-season. Rates are very low. Austria's beautiful.

Elston Really? Have you ever been there?

Sarah Well, actually, no. I myself, I have never been to Austria. But my clients have told me. And of course, I've seen photographs.

Elston   There'd be skiing accidents. Broken bones. You'd have to consider that.

Sarah   I'm not following you, Mister Jonas.

Elston   In Austria. Mountains. Skiing.

Sarah   But you wouldn't have to ski. Not necessarily.

Elston   Good point. Chances are, though, that I'd *see* an accident. Mountains everywhere. I'd be surrounded.

Sarah   Well. There are cities. Vienna, for instance. I don't think there are any mountains in Vienna. Not within city limits.

Elston   It's intensely clean there, isn't it?

Sarah   I think I've heard that.

Elston   You can't trust a place that clean. You live in a filthy place, you can't ever really get used to a sparkling clean place, can you?

Sarah   I guess not.

Elston   Have you ever tried? To live in a clean place?

Sarah   I've lived in New York all my life. I suppose that means I've lived in filth and filth alone.

Elston   Well, I tried. Once I moved to Utah. The Salt Lake's out there. But Utah was religious. And I don't trust that, either. Religious peoples harbour the strangest notions, don't you think? Especially Mormons. And Catholics. Are you Catholic?

Sarah   Yes. As a matter of fact.

Elston   I could tell by your name. Casey. Good Catholic name. My wife says I snoop. I'm sorry. Tell me if I snoop. My wife, she would like to go someplace warm that has a casino. She likes to gamble. But me, I like to sit and shiver.

Sarah   How about if I could find you someplace cold. With a casino. Best of both worlds, no?

Elston   My wife's name is Natasha. She's not Russian. But she has a Russian name. I find that odd. Her father's favourite writer was Dostoevsky and he believed he was naming her after a character. I have a joke with Natasha. If we ever have a kid, we promise to call it Raskolnikov.

Elston *laughs.* **Sarah** *doesn't.*

Elston   Raskolnikov. Get it? *Crime and Punishment.* The book.

Sarah   I've heard of it.

Elston   Dostoevsky wrote it, see? It's about . . . well, here I go babbling. Babble, babble. That's what I do. I'm so limited in what I can say to other people at my own job that I just . . . go overboard with anybody else I meet. Sorry. I'm a bankruptcy trustee.

Sarah   That's . . . really interesting.

Elston   Oh, but it's not. It's heart-breaking. I take things away from people in order to provide them with a false sense of renewal. When you take something from somebody, it stays took. They don't understand that. I do. (*Beat.*) How about Alaska? You been there?

Sarah   No. I haven't. However . . . it is cold. And there might be gambling.

Elston   Bingo halls. Of course. Eskimo bingo parlours. Or perhaps I'm thinking of the Indians. (*Beat.*) You're very well-spoken. For a travel agent.

Sarah   Thanks. I guess.

Elston   It's a gift. Take me, for example. Here I am, chirp chirp chirping away at you, and I don't consider myself to be particularly adept at the gift of gab.

Sarah   It's . . . I'm in a people job.

Elston   Hmmm. But then, so am I. Difference being that in your people job, you give them things. Information, accommodation. The potential for snapshots. Me, I remove things from people. Information, accommodation. Cash.

Sarah   Mister Jonas. Have you decided on a European vacation this year?

Elston   Oh. Oh, I am sorry. I think I'm being gracious but what I really am is a fool.

Sarah   I didn't mean that. Time. That's all. Time's a-wasting.

Elston   Oh, yes. I understand. Tick tock. Miss Casey. The most well-spoken travel agent I've ever met. But you're not well-travelled, are you?

Sarah   Well. No. I'm not . . . well-travelled.

Elston   Gosh. That's really strange. I mean, how can you s⸍ᶦᶦ airline tickets if you've never been on an airplane?

Sarah   I've been on airplanes. I have. But. It's true, I've never been abroad.

Elston   Would you like to go abroad?

Sarah   Yes. Very much. I'd like to see . . . Winchester.

Elston   An odd place for a young person to choose.

Sarah   Well, you know, there's that song. You know. (*She sings.*) Winchester Cathedral, you're bringing me –

Elston   You have a lovely singing voice, Miss Casey.

Sarah   Oh God, no. I don't. But thanks.

Elston   Do you sing in the shower?

Sarah   Pardon?

Elston   I do. Secret singers. Singing in showers. I sing Yma Sumac in the shower. Who do you sing?

Sarah   I . . . sing along. To different songs. There's this bar I go to. You know, a neighbourhood place in the Forties, near the highway and –

Elston   East or West?

Sarah   What?

Elston   Direction. Direction is important in travel. Precision. So. There's a neighbourhood bar in the Forties. East or West?

Sarah   West. On the highway, actually.

Elston   Of course. Sorry. Don't mind me. I'm an interrupter. By nature.

Sarah   Yeah. So. That's where I sing. In this bar. Sometimes I think it's open only for me to wander in and sing. Hardly anybody else goes there. Just me and Jack, he's the owner. I mean, sometimes a bum'll wander in and I give him a candy bar. Or something.

Elston   You're a kind soul.

Sarah   Nah. I just like to see people once in a while. People I don't know.

Elston   But in your job, you see people you don't know all the time.

Sarah   It's different. Here I talk about departures and arrivals. At the bar, I talk about . . . singing. Drinking. You know.

Elston   I do know. It must be sad having a job where there's no psychic stability. Always coming or going. Never staying put. The travel motif.

Sarah   Oh, sure. And you know what? When I'm in the bar with Jack and I listen to the tunes – he's got a really nice old Wurlitzer, only plays sixties tunes? Sixties tunes are the best, 'cause I know I was meant to be my age now, except I was meant to be my age in the sixties. Once, I woke up and I knew all lyrics to all songs written in the 1960s. Creepy.

Elston   Yes. I see.

Sarah   And I think, hey Sarah, whatcha doing being alive in the nineties? You missed the boat, girl. There's no going back. And then I get sad.

Elston   I find it interesting, metaphorical perhaps, that you work here. If you're around travellers enough, you'll become one yourself. And travel right back into the 1960s.

Sarah   Well. Not exactly. Christ, no. Don't get me wrong. I'm basically a happy person. I got a job. I gotta boy.

Anthony. He's sweet but he's dumb. Big hearted. A hairdresser.

Elston   Got a.

Sarah   What?

Elston   Got a. Not gotta. Enunciation, Miss Sarah Casey. (*Beat.*) I like that phrase. Its implications. Christ, no.

Sarah   Yeah. Whatever. (*Beat.*) It's time. We picked a place. For you and your wife.

Elston   I hope you don't mind me correcting you.

Sarah   No. No, you're right.

Elston   It's just that you're so well-spoken. Generally.

Sarah   Absolutely. I should . . . pay attention. To things. Like that.

Elston   So. Let's see. Where to go? You pick.

Sarah   I can't do that. It's your vacation.

Elston   But you've been such a help already. And I don't especially care where I go. What's important is the travel itself. Here. I've brought this.

Elston *gives* **Sarah** *a map.*

Sarah   It's a map of the New York metropolitan area. New Jersey. Connecticut.

Elston   Well. There is the theory that the closer one stays to home, the further one actually travels. Emily Dickinson.

Sarah   What about her?

Elston   She proves the theory. She never left home. But she travelled. Frequently. (*Beat. He points to the map.*) Pick a place. Go on. Close your eyes and let your fingers do the walking.

Sarah   You know, if I do that, you might wind up in some truly awful place.

Elston   A vacation is what you make of it. A snapshot of a landfill can be just as rewarding as a snapshot of the Eiffel Tower.

A long beat, then **Sarah** *closes her eyes and picks a place on the map. She opens her eyes, and she and* **Elston** *ponder her choice.*

Elston   Seems I'm to spend my vacation in the Holland Tunnel.

Sarah   I could pick again.

Elston   Please don't. I believe in fate. And not in coincidence. Don't you?

Five

Elston *at* **Natalie**'s *apartment.* **Elston** *holds out a box of chocolates to* **Natalie**. *He's dressed as he was in Scene One.*

Elston   It's Fannie Farmer. Sorry. I meant to bring something else. But things weren't open. This being Sunday.

Natalie   I love chocolate, Elston. Thank you.

Elston   It's embarrassing, though. Even I know it's cheap chocolate.

Natalie   Well. It's the thought that counts.

Elston (*doesn't give her the chocolate; she clocks this*)   Yes.

Natalie   How's the shop? I know I haven't been around lately but . . . this cold. Can't seem to shake it.

Elston   It's the time of year. For colds.

Natalie   Yes. Yes, it is. (*Beat.*) So. The shop. It's doing well?

Elston   It's heavy on donations. Will you allow me to take you to dinner?

Natalie   No. Thank you. I have plans.

Elston   You're the kind of person who has plans. I'm not.

Natalie   Oh, I don't have too many plans. I go with the flow.

Elston I wish I could go with the flow. But I can't. I read too much.

Natalie Well. Reading's . . . a good thing. To do.

Elston I mean, I'm not criticizing my job. You were kind to give me work. But it's not a fast-paced environment. I don't mind. I have time to read. Magazines. Trade magazines. You would not believe the number of different professions out there, Natalie. And each profession has a trade magazine. Why do you suppose they're called trade magazines?

Natalie Look. I really don't know.

Elston There's no barter system involved. It's not like, I trade you money for clothes. It's all about taking. Not trading. Don't you think?

Natalie You're absolutely right, Elston. It's all about taking. So. How about I take the week's receipts from you?

Elston Laura sends her best.

Natalie Great. Send her mine.

Elston Wouldn't you like to meet her? I mean, she knows how much you've done for me. She admires you.

Natalie Meeting Laura would be . . . nice. Sometime.

Elston We're going to be married. In the fall. I saw a travel agent two weeks ago and arranged the trip. We're going through the Holland Tunnel. By car. I wish we could take a train, though. I love trains. And people who travel. Don't you?

Natalie When you work, it's hard to travel.

Elston But you don't work. You own.

Natalie Still. I've got to keep an eye on things, don't I?

Elston Do you feel you've got to keep an eye on me?

Natalie No. That is not what I meant. I mean to say that ownership is a great responsibility.

Elston   I see what you mean. Like the slaves. That was a great responsibility, keeping an eye on so many people.

Natalie   The receipts. Give me the receipts, Elston.

Elston   Laura's on tour this week. That's why I have a free night and why I thought you might . . . she's a tennis player. Did I tell you that?

Natalie   You might have. I don't really remember.

Elston   She's never won a tournament but she's in constant motion. I love athletes, don't you? Such grace under pressure. Such skill. I am completely unskilled. Have you ever noticed that about me?

Natalie   Yes. Yes, I – no. I didn't mean to suggest –

Elston   Laura's a pretty girl. Tall. Taller than me. A redhead. Freckles. Thin ankles. I like that in a woman. The kind of ankle that looks like it would break if you so much as blow on it. We were high-school sweethearts. In Idaho. She was the prom queen. I wasn't the king. But she preferred me to all the others. I was in science club. I looked at things. Under slides. Glass makes things look better. If people walked around pressed between two gigantic slides of glass, they'd look better, too.

Natalie   ELSTON. (*Beat.*) Please. The receipts. I need the receipts.

Elston *gives* **Natalie** *a large envelope.* **Natalie** *looks through it.*

Natalie   This is good, Elston. Very neat. You've done well this week. Thank you.

Elston   Natalie is a beautiful name.

Natalie   Well, yes. It is. Thank you.

Elston   A real spy name. My wife Natasha has a spy name and I'm forever telling her –

Natalie   What? What did you say?

Elston   I was saying. I was. My sister. She's . . . never mind.

Natalie   You said your wife. Natasha.

Elston   Did I? I'm thinking of Laura. Would you possibly travel with me?

Natalie   I think you should leave now. I do have plans.

Elston   I feel the urge to have plans. Let's travel to dinner. I don't know much about you, Natalie, but I would like to know. Everything.

Natalie   Our relationship prohibits. It.

Elston   Do we have a relationship?

Natalie   Yes. I'm your employer. I employ you.

Elston   I like that. I work for you. I belong to you.

Natalie   I wouldn't go that far.

Elston   I meant it figuratively. I love language. Don't you? I'm all dressed up with no place to go. Won't you let me buy you dinner? Let me spend money on you.

A telephone rings. It rings again. A beat.

Natalie   Excuse me, Elston. Don't touch – just stay put. All right?

Natalie *exits. Telephone rings again. And again. A silence.*

Elston (*as if* **Natalie**'s *still there*)   I'm a magician. Really. Me and a girl named Blue, we do the New England carnival circuit. Did I tell you that? I have a special trick that nobody else does. Let me show you.

He takes a box of matches out of his pocket. He lights one, holds it between his thumb and forefinger. It burns down to his fingers. He doesn't flinch.

People faint when they see this trick. It doesn't hurt. It never hurts. It never hurts. (*Beat.*) I love fire. The way it travels. Don't you? Let me show you another trick.

*He unwraps the box of chocolates. He eats them at a rapid pace,
stuffing them into his mouth.*

Excess. Excess is my encore. It's astonishing.

Natalie *enters. She watches* **Elston** *eating chocolates.*

Elston (*notices* **Natalie**) I was hungry.

Natalie I'm running late. You'll have to go.

Elston How can you go out on a date if you have a cold
you can't shake?

Natalie Watch me and see.

Elston When will you go to dinner with Laura and me?

Natalie Some other time, Ellie. When I don't have any
plans.

Elston But you always have plans.

Natalie Yes. I do.

Elston So that means you don't go with the flow. You said
you did. Could I ask you for a raise?

Natalie Ask me some other time.

Elston When? When shall I ask you?

Natalie Soon. We'll talk.

Elston We will? Good. Because there are some things I'd
like to ask you. For instance, why is it called a thrift shop?
Seems to me it ought to be called a generosity shop. You
know?

Natalie I'll have to think about that one. Later.

Elston Have you ever been to New Jersey?

Natalie No. And I don't ever want to go. Leave now.
Please. I really have to get out –

Elston Isn't it funny how you can live in a place for years
and there's this other place right over a river yet you never

seem to get there? (*Beat.*) You called me Ellie. Before. Why'd
you do that?

Six

Jack *and* **Ellen** *at their press conference.* **Ted Mitchell** *and*
Timothy Creighton *watch them.*

Ellen (*tapping her microphone*)   Is this on? Hello, hello. One
small step for man, one giant leap for mankind. Testing.
One. Two. Three. Hello. Ladies and gentlemen of the press:
this is the press conference. With me is Jack Fallon, the
bartender who, as far as we know, is the last person to have
seen my Sarah before she . . . went away. What's that? Well.
No. We don't know that she exactly went away.

Jack   We sure don't.

Ellen   Mister Fallon will now make his statement.

Jack   This is my statement: listen, buddy. We want her
back. Come back, Sarah. (*Beat.*) That's all.

Ellen   What's that, miss? Nope. Haven't heard a thing. No
ransom notes. And it's a good thing, too, 'cause I ain't got
any money. I'm ordinary. YOU HEAR ME, YOU SKINNY
CREEP? I GOT NO MONEY. (*Beat.*) I have some pictures
of Sarah from happier times.

She displays baby photos.

See? All smiles. And to think she might be, at this very
moment, stuffed in a trunk or bound and gagged and forced
to – well. A mother's private grief is best not spread over the
airwaves.

Jack   Mrs Casey ain't feeling well, fellas. What? No. No, I
can't talk to you about that night on the advice of the New
York City Police Department. Can't give away details of
what you might call the perp's *modus operandi*. Huh? No. I
ain't got no book deals out of this. And the bar's open, guys.

Round the clock. I got my mother working days. Just in case, you know, the asshole's stupid enough to come back. I'm offering my Golden Gloves trophies to anybody who comes into the bar with information leading to the arrest of the perp. How's that?

Ellen I just wanna say: honey, come home. I'm keeping a candle in the window so you can see our satellite antenna guiding your way. Your room is untouched by human hands. Except, you know, mine. I boughtcha a new record. See?

She holds up a 45 r.p.m. record.

Cost a bundle, so you better come back and listen to it. I hoped you was gonna be a nurse so you could patch up the mess I – I can't. I can't go on. The stress. The sleepless nights. What's that? No. I don't got no current pictures of Sarah. We stopped taking pictures when the Polaroid broke. No. No graduation photos. I wasn't there. Look. It wasn't a big deal.

Ted Mitchell *steps forward.*

Ted Thank you, Mrs Casey. At this time, we'd like to announce that we have located Timothy Creighton, who had been identified as the man with whom Sarah Casey left O'Malley's Saloon on the evening of the thirteenth. Mr Creighton, would you please step forward?

Timothy Creighton *inches forward.* **Ellen** *and* **Jack** *watch him.*

Jack That ain't him.

Ted We know.

Timothy (*at a microphone*) My name is Timothy Creighton. I was not in O'Malley's Saloon on the night of the thirteenth. I've never been to O'Malley's Saloon. In fact, I've never been west of Fifth Avenue. Nor do I plan an excursion west of Fifth Avenue in the foreseeable future. I am an entertainment attorney. I am forty-three years old. My wife, a research biologist, and my three sons are my pride and joy. I have been, from time to time, a Little League coach. I have never met Sarah Casey and really, I don't plan to meet her. In the foreseeable future. Though, of course, I and my entire family, wish her well and expect that she will return to her . . . mother . . . soon. I am – I am disturbed. By the incessant media crush I've been subjected to. My doorman, regrettably, has fallen prey to the temptation of easy cash and so several of you have been permitted to camp inside my building's lobby. And my wife swears that some of you have watched her doing laundry in our basement. Thus, Detective Mitchell and I have decided the time is right. For me to come forward. I am not involved in any way in this case. Nor do I know who might be. Please. Leave us alone. Contrary to published reports, I am not part of a satanic ritual abuse cult. I do not make human sacrifices. My wife was never involved in a day-care scandal and yes, my children are my own. Let me repeat: I am not a criminal. I'm just . . . tired of getting funny looks from my greengrocer. I'm afraid to go to my barber. Please. Understand this. Thank you.

Timothy *exits.*

Ted (*to* **Ellen** *and* **Jack**)   He's given us a name.

Jack   What name?

Ted   A name. Of a man. There might be a connection.

Ellen   He seems like such a nice man.

Ted   Mrs Casey. We have a lead. A good one.

Ellen   Lead? What lead? My daughter's dead. (*Beat, then back to the press corps.*) I'm crocheting a new blanket for Sarah so it's ready for her. When she comes home.

Seven

Music in: 'Paper Doll' (The Mills Brothers). **Sarah** *and* **Anthony** *dance.* **Sarah** *tries to teach* **Anthony** *to waltz, but it's really the wrong song to be using.* **Sarah** *is dressed as she was in Scene One.* **Ellen** *reads a tabloid.*

Anthony   Hey. Gimme a break, Sarah. This music sucks for dancing.

Sarah   It's not so bad. It's old. I like old things.

Anthony   Yeah. Like your mother.

Ellen   Hey. Shit for brains. Watchya mouth.

Anthony   Mrs Casey, you ever dance to this stuff?

Ellen   Leave me alone. I'm reading. I'm learning things.

Anthony   Yeah? What things?

Ellen   Important things.

Sarah   Ma. You don't learn anything by reading stuff like that. Read a book. A newspaper.

Ellen   I watch TV for my news. I like the colour commentary.

Anthony   Mrs Casey, you know how to waltz?

Ellen   Sure. Sarah's pig of a father taught me when he was drunk. He thought he was Christopher Plummer and I was Julie Andrews in *The Sound of Music*. He tried to re-enact the gazebo scene. It didn't work. But wouldn't that be nice? A gazebo. I've always wanted one.

Sarah   You can't have a gazebo in the city, Ma.

Ellen   Why not? People got shrines, don't they? I want a gazebo. Hey Anthony: you gonna buy me a gazebo?

Anthony   Yeah. When your daughter marries me.

Sarah   Great. Like I'm some fucking dowry for a gazebo.

Ellen   Marry him already. Get it over with.

Sarah   I'd rather he learned to waltz.

Ellen   What? So you can dance at the wedding?

Sarah   No. That's not why.

Ellen   What the fuck are you talking about? Nobody dances once they're married.

Anthony   Hey, Mrs Casey. Watchya mouth.

Ellen   You big asshole. Shut up. Cut my hair. Ain't that what you do? Cut hair?

Anthony   You want a haircut now?

Ellen   Fucking right. Come over here and make me beautiful.

Anthony *tends to* **Ellen**'s *hair throughout the remainder of the scene.*

Sarah   I can't believe this, Anthony. You promised.

Anthony   I kept my promise. We danced.

Sarah   Don't cut her hair. Let's go out.

Anthony   You wanna go to the movies?

Sarah   No. I just . . . wanna go. Downtown. To the Village. I want a double espresso.

Anthony   I can make you a double espresso. Besides, you know I don't feel right in those café places. Lotsa guys, you know, talking about foreign films and stuff.

Sarah   What's wrong with that?

Anthony   Nothing. If you're a foreigner.

Sarah   I hate you sometimes, Anthony. I really do.

Ellen   A perfect way to enter marriage. With rage. Go on. Do it. I waited until my rage at your father was gone before I married him. And look at what an uninteresting life we led. May he rest in peace.

Sarah   I don't want to get married. İ want to travel.

Anthony   Fine. We'll go to Sicily on our honeymoon. My grandma's got a big house with those French windows.

Sarah   I don't want to visit your grandmother. I want to visit Italy.

Anthony   Sicily's Italy. I speak the language. Don't worry.

Sarah   I DON'T LIKE YOUR GRANDMOTHER.

Ellen   I'll go with you, Anthony. We get there, you sit me in a garden, give me a jug of red wine, you go off and do your business. I need a vacation.

Sarah   Anthony. Come out with me. Now.

Anthony   Say you'll marry me and I'll come out with you.

Sarah   I don't want to marry you.

Ellen   And just who does she think she's gonna marry?

Anthony   She's playing hard to get.

Ellen   I played hard to get once. And what did it get me? Got me a man who thought he was a member of the Von Trapp family singers. Take a hint from your mother, girlie. Marry this guy. He's got his own business.

Anthony (*to* **Sarah**)   I love you, babe.

Sarah   Jesus. Fuck you all. I'm too young to get married.

Ellen   You know, Anthony, she's been this way since she's been taking night classes at Pace.

Anthony   Yeah? I didn't notice no changes.

Ellen   Oh, I notice the changes. She speaks in tongues. You oughtta hear it.

Sarah   I'm studying Greek, Ma.

Ellen   Yeah, well. Whatever it is, I can't read it. And if I can't read it, cook it or hit it, I don't trust it. Do me a favour, Sarah. Just *say* you'll marry him.

Anthony   We're gonna have a great reception. My brother's band is gonna play. We'll have it at this place out in Flatbush.

Sarah   I won't get married in Flatbush.

Ellen   What? You'd rather get married here? See, Anthony? I think Sarah has this hunch she's gonna marry some Hollywood type. Kinda guy she can speak in tongues to. But look. Look at what I'm reading. It says that everybody in

California is dying from cancer. See? So it don't do you no good to leave home.

Anthony I hadda uncle who went to California. San Diego. There's some kinda really big aquarium and it was his lifelong dream to go there and see the whales. So he saves and saves his money – which he was doing for a long time, 'cause he was a hot-dog vendor at Yankee Stadium – and finally he gets the cash together for the trip. He don't tell nobody he's going, 'cause it's like something he's been dreaming of his whole life and you don't share that stuff with anybody. So one night, he just disappears to San Diego. Turns up at Sea World. And what happens is, the place is closed. The first time in its history the place is closed for renovations. My uncle's, like, booked this two-week trip. So what does he do? Every day for two weeks he leaves his motel and drives to the gates. Stands there all day long. Fucking old guy trying to glimpse a whale through gates.

Sarah I don't want to hear any more stories about life's little disappointments, Anthony.

Ellen Be quiet, you. Go on, Anthony. I like this story. It's soothing.

Anthony You're not gonna believe what happens to him.

Ellen What? Don't tell me. The whale, using an animal's ESP, senses your uncle's presence and swims up to the gates?

Sarah You're sick.

Anthony No, wait. Wait. So. On his last night, he's frantic. He's gotta leave the next morning. And he knows he ain't ever gonna be able to afford the trip again, cause, like he's seventy-seven goddamned years old. So. On that last night, he starts climbing the gate. Scales it, like he's a teenager or something. He gets to the top and for a single second, I guess he can see the whales. Then, like that: ba-bing. He slips at the edge, impales himself on the top of the gate. Ba-boom. Clean shot. Right through the heart. Poor fuck.

Ellen At least he didn't stay in California long enough to catch the cancer.

Sarah   You two are pathetic. That's a really charming story, Anthony. I guess there's some lesson attached to it? A moral?

Anthony   Lesson? Who said anything about a lesson? I'm asking you to marry me, Sarah.

Ellen   The lesson is this: don't go nowhere without calling ahead to see if it's open. That means you, Sarah.

Sarah   I'm not calling nobody. Europe's always open, Ma. Countries don't close.

Ellen   Yes they do. Fucking Russians closed their country.

Sarah   Guess what? IT'S OPEN AGAIN. Read something. LEARN SOMETHING.

Ellen   Look you little bitch: I know more than you're ever gonna know. You got your father's attitude oh miss high and mighty stuck up bastard daughter of a mick NO GOOD FUCK. I know all I need to know about how to get through THINGS.

Anthony   Hey hey – chill out, Mrs Casey. I got the scissors right here. Don't wanna hurt you.

Ellen   Go ahead. Hurt me. I won't notice. I got a daughter who uses me for a doormat. Wipes her feet all over my GUTS. I'M SORRY I DON'T GOT THE KEYS TO FUCKING PARIS FRANCE IN MY POCKET.

Sarah   Anthony, you wanna know what I did in school on Friday?

Ellen   GO ON. HURT ME. SUE ME.

Sarah   Answer me, Anthony.

Anthony   Yeah, yeah babe. I do. If I listen to what you did at college, wouldja marry me? Wouldja?

Sarah   I'm going out.

Ellen   Yeah? Whereya going on a Sunday night?

Sarah   I'm going to Russia. There's a train leaving Grand Central any minute. (*Beat.*) I'll be at O'Malley's.

Ellen   Oh. Little booze-bag.

Sarah   Bitch. You make me wanna give up. You hear that? I sit here with the two of you, and you make me want to GIVE UP. I sit here too long and it's like tendrils grow up my legs, like I'm being rooted here.

Ellen   That's because you can't communicate. That's because you're moody.

Sarah   It's in my genes.

Anthony   What's in your jeans, babe? You restless?

Sarah   Yeah. I'm restless. I wanna talk to Jack. He always listens.

Ellen   And I don't?

Sarah   I'll be at O'Malley's. (*Beat.*) Don't wait up.

Eight

Elston *at the thrift shop. He wears boxer shorts. He's surrounded by clothes, which he sorts through. There's a full-length mirror nearby.*

Elston (*holds up a pair of trousers*)   Thank you, Mister Harris. Thank you for the wool. When it's cold, wool's best. Unless you have cashmere. But who can afford it? Mister Harris, I hope you and your wife are warm tonight. I hope you are huddled together and sipping champagne by candlelight. I hope you have a fireplace. I hope your children are asleep and dreaming of a time when they'll be free to travel. I hope they're never ill. I hope you remember me.

He puts on the trousers. He holds up a shirt.

And thank you, Mister Chester Ingalls, for this cotton. It's a very fine English shirt. I hope you're in London now. I hope you're relaxing in a five-star hotel in Knightsbridge. I hope you're not afraid of leaving your home after dark. I hope you never tire of giving away your old clothes. I hope you remember me.

He puts on the shirt. He holds up a jacket.

And where would I be without you, Mister Holloway? This jacket is a magnificent piece of tailoring. The very finest silk and linen. The mixture is exquisite. I fear you're full of rage. I hope you don't beat your girlfriend. I hope she agrees to the house in Westbury. I hope that one day you will hop a commuter train to that house and there she'll be. Waiting for you at the station in a red Volvo. I hope you never declare bankruptcy. I hope you remember me.

He puts on the jacket. He examines himself in the mirror.

For what is a man without his friends?

Ted Mitchell *enters.*

Ted   Elston Rupp?

Elston   Yes.

Ted   The door was open. The front door.

Elston   Yes.

Ted   I'm Ted Mitchell. NYPD. Homicide division.

Elston   Yes.

Ted   I'd like to ask you some questions. Would you . . . come with me?

Elston   Yes.

Ted   Shall we go?

Elston   Do you have a car?

Ted   Yes. The car's outside. Out front.

Elston   I love cars. (*Beat.*) Take me someplace.

Elston *holds his hands out in front of his body, as if to be handcuffed.*

Blackout.

Act Two

Nine

Ted Mitchell *interviews* **Elston**.

Elston Is this the place where you question criminals?

Ted Sometimes.

Elston It looks like that kind of place. I've never been to one of those places. But. This has the feel of a place where people experience fear.

Ted Are you experiencing fear?

Elston Oh, no. No. I trust you. You took me someplace.

Ted You like to travel.

Elston Yes, I do. But I don't often get the chance. Work. Family obligations.

Ted You told me you don't have a family.

Elston That doesn't mean I don't have obligations. To family. We carry obligation with us, Ted. Regardless.

Ted You had family. Once. Tell me about them.

Elston Am I under arrest?

Ted No.

Elston Do you have a family?

Ted Everybody does.

Elston And do you feel obligated to them?

Ted Tell me some more about Sarah Casey.

Elston A lovely girl. A travel agent. Do you know she never went anywhere?

Ted No. I didn't. How do you know that?

Elston She told me.

Ted When? When did she tell you that?

Elston   When did you become a detective?

Ted   Did Sarah Casey tell you she never travelled before or after you left O'Malley's? (*Beat.*) I became a detective six years ago.

Elston   Did you have to shoot somebody to become a detective?

Ted   No, Elston. It doesn't work that way.

Elston   Did you have to go to a special school?

Ted   No. No special school. Tell me more about Sarah Casey.

Elston   Sarah Casey went to school. But she didn't need any particular skills to become a travel agent. Just like you don't need particular skills to be a detective.

Ted   I answered some questions for you. Now, you answer some for me.

Elston   Give and take. I give, you take. Am I under arrest?

Ted   No. Should you be?

Elston   I have many friends. Natalie's my best friend.

Ted   I know. She told me that.

Elston   When did she tell you that?

Ted   Oh, about the same time Sarah Casey was telling you about her lack of travel skills.

A silence.

Elston   Natalie has nice ankles. Did she show you them?

Ted   She showed me her ledgers. Said you kept them up well. Said you're a good worker. Solid. Honest. Are you honest?

Elston   I'm taking Natalie to dinner next week. She's very busy. But she made time for me.

Ted   Did you have dinner with Sarah Casey?

Elston   When? When are we talking? I need times. I do better. With a little direction. That's why I'm such a good worker.

Ted   That Sunday.

Elston   That Sunday. (*Beat.*) No. No dinner with Sarah Casey.

Ted   But you did leave O'Malley's with her.

Elston   Yes. Yes, I did.

Ted   And then?

Elston   I went home.

Ted   And what about Sarah?

Elston   She's lovely. A travel agent. I love to travel. Am I under arrest?

Ted   No. (*Beat.*) I love to travel.

Elston   Do you? You must drive a lot. Being a detective.

Ted   Did you know that the average detective logs more miles per annum than the average cabbie?

Elston   Yes. I do know that. Maps. You must have lots of maps.

Ted   Oh, sure. I had a special glove compartment built to accommodate all my maps. I like roads.

Elston   Yes. And there are many, many roads in this country. Aren't there?

Ted   Yup. Roads are necessary for travel. And for what else?

Elston   Sightseeing. Speedy exits.

Ted   That's the interesting part. Speedy exits.

Elston   You sound like you know what I'm talking about, Ted.

Ted   Yes. Fast cars. Starless nights. Blind alleys. Places to hide. Speedy exits.

Elston If you drive so much, you should know what I'm talking about. That's not what I'm talking about.

Ted Educate me, Elston. Please.

Elston I observe speed limits. Actually, I always drive in the right lane. With the old people. Except for the exits. On exit ramps, I accelerate. Fifty, sixty, seventy. Someday I'd like to take an exit ramp at eighty.

Ted Isn't that dangerous?

Elston I don't know. Maybe.

Ted If you think it might be dangerous, then why do you do it?

Elston I get excited when I anticipate arriving. At a destination. Having a family is dangerous, too.

Ted Maybe.

Elston Well. If you think it might be dangerous, then why do you do it?

Ted Do you own a car, Elston? Did you maybe take Sarah Casey for a ride?

Elston I take cabs. I like cabs. Do you know, I won't take a cab unless it has a plexiglass barrier inside to separate passenger and driver? (*Beat.*) I used to drive. But I've never owned a car, Ted.

Ted We've been at this for two hours. Did you know that?

Elston Yes. It's been very pleasant. Did Natalie tell you she didn't like me? Because I wouldn't like to spend money on a woman who doesn't like me.

Ted You like money.

Elston No. I don't. That's why I spend it.

Ted Did you spend any money on Sarah Casey?

Elston Oh, no. I barely know her. Though she likes me. I would spend money on her. She's kind. Are you kind, Ted?

Ted   All right, Elston. These are the things I know about you: You like to travel. You won't ride in certain taxis. You're a good worker who keeps an honest ledger. You met Sarah Casey at O'Malley's last Sunday evening. You left the bar with her. You're taking Natalie to dinner. Give me something else. Sarah Casey has disappeared.

Elston   Good for her. She deserves to go. Away. She's never been anywhere.

Ted   Did you take her anywhere?

Elston   Well. I told her that there was the possibility. Of going away.

Ted   You have a fiancée named Laura.

Elston   Laura is a tennis player.

Ted   I know. She's never won a match.

Elston   She's never won a tournament.

Ted   There's one thing, though, Elston. About Laura. We can't find her.

Elston   Perhaps she went away.

Ted   We can find no evidence that she actually exists.

Elston   You know, Ted, when I was a boy, people went away a lot. And they never came back.

Ted   People who go away generally leave a trail.

Elston   Are you going to arrest me?

Ted   Tell me why you posed as Tim Creighton last Sunday night.

Elston   Because I wore his clothes.

Ted   You told Jack Fallon and Sarah Casey that you were a killer.

Elston   I also told them I was Timothy J. Creighton. Ted. Why won't you arrest me?

Ted   I will ask you once more. Why. Why did you tell those people you were a killer?

Elston   Because they believed me. Because. Haven't you ever wanted to be anybody else, Ted?

Ted   Never. Why do you want to be somebody else?

Elston   Because I'm more honest than you. I know. Who I actually am. Do you? (*Beat.*) Arrest me. Please.

Ted   Are you a killer?

Elston   Have you ever shot anyone on the job?

Ted   Not yet.

Elston   But don't you want to? Don't you? If you don't have an urge to use your gun, why do you carry it? Shoot me.

Ted   That's enough. That's – look. I'll tell you something. I admit it. I don't like my job. I don't especially like the company I'm keeping lately. I don't like you. I might be doing other things. I might have swum the English Channel. I might have been a priest.

Elston   I wish you were a priest, Ted. I wish I had something to confess.

Ted   I really couldn't care less for a confession. I want to believe that you are just another sad bastard who's got a thing for wearing other people's cast-offs. I want to believe that you lead the same fucking boring life I lead. That the worst thing you've ever done is short-change Natalie a few bucks on the week's take. Tell me you're dull, Elston. Tell me what I want to hear. Help me see this through.

Elston   You're an unhappy man, Ted. You need a vacation. You need to travel.

Ted   If you've got nothing to do with that girl's disappearance, why didn't you contact us?

Elston   I didn't know you were looking for me.

Ted   It's been all over the news.

Elston   I don't have a TV. Or a radio. I don't read newspapers.

Ted   You know an awful lot of trivia for somebody who doesn't pay attention to the media.

Elston   I said I don't read newspapers. I do pay attention. I do.

Ted   Did you kill Sarah Casey?

Elston   No. Did you? Is that why you're so unhappy?

Ted *grabs* **Elston**.

Ted   Listen you little sonofabitch: HELP ME.

Elston   You don't want me to be guilty. I can tell.

Ted   I don't give a good goddamn if you're guilty. GIVE ME SOME ANSWERS.

Elston   You're kind, Ted. Like Sarah Casey. Why are you so unhappy?

Ted   I HATE MY JOB I WISH I WAS ON THE TAKE MY WIFE'S ABOUT TO LEAVE ME I REALLY DON'T CARE AND I. CANNOT STAND. MY CHILDREN.

Ted *releases* **Elston**. *A silence as* **Ted** *composes himself.*

Elston   On that night. That Sunday night. I close the shop early. I don't know why. I decide to do inventory. I come across Timothy Creighton's tuxedo. Mrs Creighton had been in earlier that week. She always dry-cleans her donations. She's one of the few to observe that rule. And it is a rule, you see. Sometimes, I break the rule and accept unwashed clothing from customers I like. I don't know why. Mrs Creighton makes regular donations. I know her first name. She doesn't know mine. She never did. I wonder if that bothers her now. I've never met Mr Creighton. I find a business card in the left breast-pocket of his tuxedo jacket. It's stained. Red wine, I think. I feel sorry for Mr Creighton. I don't know why. But in that moment, I like him very much. I have to like a person to wear his clothes. Don't you? I put on the tux. I leave the shop. It is six thirty. I go to Natalie's. I drop off the week's receipts on Sunday nights. She hadn't felt well that week. I had hoped she would allow

me to take her to dinner. She wouldn't. Allow me. I don't
know why. I leave Natalie's. I head home. I get to my front
door and I find I can't insert my key into its lock. It occurs
to me that I should go to Timothy Creighton's house. But I
don't. I don't know why. I go to O'Malley's. I don't go to
bars, but I go there. Men in bars laugh at me. Because I'm
so small. Because they're glad they're not that small. Because
I allow them to laugh. I am O'Malley's only customer that
night. I take an immediate liking to Jack Fallon. I begin to
wish that he could be my brother. And then. Sarah Casey
enters the bar. I recognize her instantly as the woman who
had helped me plan a vacation two weeks earlier. You didn't
know that, did you, Ted? I went to her travel agency. I do
that frequently. Drop by. At different travel agencies. I talk
to women who work in travel agencies. It's the only time
women are happy to speak to me. When there's the
possibility that I'll spend money in their business
establishments. I often offer to spend money on women I
know. And they never let me. I don't know why. Sarah
Casey was the last travel agent I spoke to. Of course, at the
time, I was wearing the clothing of a Paul Jonas. Poor Mister
Jonas died on the QE2 while he and his wife celebrated their
diamond jubilee. He never did get to wear his new suit. So.
Wearing the clothes of Paul Jonas, I, with the aid of Sarah
Casey, plan a vacation I never intend to take. Sarah is very
kind. I pay in cash. I buy two packet trips, via Greyhound
buses, to Atlantic City. I leave the travel agency and mean to
rip up the tickets. But I don't. I don't know why. When I see
Sarah at O'Malley's I feel it is fate. We talk. Sarah confesses
a desire to travel. I'm certain she doesn't recognize me. I
entertain her by proposing the possibility of differing
scenarios. For her life. Overall, I'm sure I present a very
attractive portrait of Timothy J. Creighton. And while I like
Sarah, I know she will not allow me to spend money on her.
She will not suggest a ride on the Circle Line. She will not.
Take a trip. With me. She tires. She wants to go home. I
open the door for her. She steps outside. I show her the
bright, full moon. I point her in the direction of the Holland
Tunnel. There is a moment when our continuing in the same

direction is possible. She takes a step. I hesitate. It makes all the difference. I watch her walk downtown. I watch her take steps. I stand perfectly still. I call out to her. Sarah, I say, Sarah Casey: where are you going? And then she disappears.

Ted (*after a silence*)   Thank you. (*Beat.*) Would you like . . . a cup of coffee?

Elston   Will you arrest me now?

Ted   Would you prefer, I don't know, tea?

Elston   Will I make you famous, Ted?

Ted   Well. I'd rather you made me rich.

Elston   I'm sorry about your wife. And your kids.

Ted   Are you?

Elston   Don't leave.

Ted   I need some coffee.

Elston   I like you, Ted. Why'd you let go of me? I liked it when you held me. I liked it.

Ten

Natalie *and* **Timothy** *at the police station. It's clear each knows who the other is, but neither wants to commit to conversation.*

Timothy   How could you hire somebody like that? There. I've said it. I had to say it.

Natalie   I'm sure I don't understand what you're talking about.

Timothy   I've never even met this man. Do you realize that? I'm here to identify a tuxedo.

Natalie   He sells old clothing for me. That's all I know. And I don't think we're supposed to be chatting right now.

Timothy   I'll probably lose my job over this.

Natalie   Well. I'm sorry.

Timothy   No. You're not sorry. You're mortified. Mortified that you're involved in this at all.

Natalie   But I'm not involved. (*Beat.*) You're the lawyer, aren't you.

Timothy   Yeah. Lucky me. Personally, I think you're the guiltiest party in this mess.

Natalie   You're much more handsome than you appear to be on television. I've seen clips of your statement. You're actually very handsome.

Timothy   Well. Thank you. (*Beat.*) I've got to ask you this. I really do. Don't you screen applications for employment? Don't you ask for references?

Natalie   This is the situation, Tim. May I call you that? May I call you Tim?

Timothy   Timothy. I prefer Timothy. Actually.

Natalie   Well then, Timothy. This is the situation. I inherit a ridiculous business from a dear but preposterous spinster aunt. I have no wish to sort through dirty old clothes. Now I ask you: Is this an unreasonable position to take? It's a charity business. How is anybody supposed to make anything of it: Nevertheless, I respect my aunt's wishes and take over this – thrift place. And who do you think I can hire for the overwhelmingly tedious job of running the hovel on a daily basis? Would you do it, Timothy? No. I thought not. Furthermore, what do you suppose I can afford to pay the lucky recipient of this position? I can hardly be picky when we're talking a minimum wage type situation. Don't you agree? Yes. I though you would. And so. How can you fault me for hiring a thoroughly agreeable – if somewhat odd – young man? He told me he was from Nebraska. He told me he was the child of farmers. He's polite. He's well-spoken. He's never stolen anything from me and he's not likely to leave his job and decide to become an artist. He took a polygraph. He passed. He's mine for life if I want him. What else should I have done? So he embellishes from time to time. He seems to have several wives and fiancées, all of whom he really can't keep straight from one conversation to the next, but . . . who am I to judge? I think he's honest. And I believe he is telling the truth about the Casey girl's disappearance. He's always on time. He makes the customers laugh. And while it's true I would not choose to be his friend, I don't think that counts as proof of anything other than that he – he makes me nervous. In fact, he makes my skin crawl. He's not the kind of man I ordinarily talk to. He's small.

Timothy You hired a man who makes your skin crawl. You hired a man who wears other people's clothing.

Natalie Well. Coming from a thrift shop perspective, I don't find that at all unusual.

Timothy You don't.

Natalie Of course not. Look, he sells other people's clothing to other people all the time. Lots of people wear other people's clothing. I had no idea he was doing . . . whatever he was doing . . . and I thoroughly object to the practice but –

Timothy You support him anyway.

Natalie I didn't say I support him.

Timothy You'll stick by him on this.

Natalie I didn't say that, either.

Timothy Most of the people I work with think I have something to do with this woman's disappearance.

Natalie Did you?

Timothy I said I didn't. The bartender said I didn't.

Natalie People lie. People are paid to lie.

Timothy You don't actually believe –

Natalie I read it. In the *Post*. It's one theory.

Timothy Oh. I missed that one.

Natalie It's very interesting. You see, the theory is that you and the bartender are in it together.

Timothy I think I've heard a variation on this.

Natalie   You take attractive young girls and sell them into the white slave-trade. In California. Evidently, it's running rampant out there. And, the theory continues, you framed Elston. You know. Made it look like he did it. Or at least raised the serious possibility that he did it.

Timothy   Did what? (*Beat.*) Look. Is it just a coincidence he was wearing my suit? Or maybe – maybe the bartender and I hit him over the head, dressed him up in my suit, dragged him to the bar, sat him on a stool and waited until he woke up? And, naturally, he'd have no memory of such an event.

Natalie   The *Post* didn't offer any details. It just made a couple of suppositions.

Timothy   I could make a couple of suppositions about you.

Natalie   No. You couldn't. My name is not being associated with, well, the more unsavoury aspects of this case.

Timothy   Like you said. People accept money. To lie.

Natalie   Meaning just what. Exactly.

Timothy   Meaning. If I lose my job, I'd maybe take some money to say a few things about you.

Natalie   Really, Tim, don't be ridiculous. You're being ridiculous.

Timothy   People stare at me when I walk my dog.

Natalie   I should be so lucky, Tim.

Timothy   I'm angry. And CALL ME TIMOTHY, GODDAMNIT.

Natalie (*after a beat*)   After this blows over, you can probably get a job anywhere. You'll be a celebrity. Who wouldn't want to hire somebody like you? The office gossip would be extraordinary. But what about me? All I'm left with is the same no-win business situation. What do you think I can do? Hang a sign outside: THIS IS THE PLACE WHERE IT MIGHT HAVE HAPPENED?

Timothy   My privacy has been violated.

Natalie   Whose hasn't? Sell your story. Beat them to the punch.

Timothy   He was wearing my clothes. He might have killed a woman while he wore my tuxedo.

Natalie   And she might have simply walked away. You know, this is not exactly the Lindbergh case. Grown corpses really are hard to conceal. Not to mention there's been no evidence, none whatever, to connect Elston to anything other than having worn a tuxedo that didn't fit him.

Timothy   People look at me and they see a criminal. And I cannot stop feeling guilty for something that somebody else did while I was holding my wife in my arms.

Natalie   I just thought of something funny. You're here to identify a tuxedo. It's like identifying a body, except it's not. Isn't that funny?

Timothy   Why are you here?

Natalie   Oh. Well, Elston. He had nobody else to pick him up.

Timothy   He's here? He's in this building now?

Natalie   Yes. I think I'll do something nice for him this evening. Like take him to dinner. (*Beat*.) Unless of course you'd rather come out to dinner with me. After you identify the tuxedo.

Timothy   No. Thank you. I have . . . reading. To catch up on. (*Beat*.) Would you do me a favour? Would you . . . tell me you don't believe I have anything to do with this? Because I'm beginning to doubt myself. Sometimes. Sometimes I think, well, what if. What if my wife hadn't cleaned out our closets that day. What if I had been home to stop her from giving away that tux. It didn't fit me any more. But I liked it. You hold on to things that mean something to you.

Natalie   I'm afraid I can't sympathize. I try not to wear anything more than once if I can help it.

Timothy   Somebody's daughter is missing and possibly dead. And I can't escape the feeling that she, well, that she saw me that night. Or a part of me. I can't . . . say anything else. About it.

Natalie   Okay. I don't believe you had anything to do with this. (*Beat.*) Now. Why don't you come out with me for a drink? You really are a good-looking man. Much better looking than you appear to be. On television, I mean.

Eleven

Ted, **Ellen** *and* **Anthony** *at* **Ellen**'*s apartment,* **Ellen** *holds a half-crocheted blanket.*

Ted   It's an empty room on the highway between Forty-Fourth and Forty-Fifth. Not a bed. Not a chair. Not one stick of furniture. Just . . . globes. Of every conceivable size and description. A globe of the moon. Of Mars. A geopolitical globe. A population density globe. And one file cabinet. Full of five-by-seven unlined white notepads. And on these notepads, neat rows of dates and times. No names. Just descriptions. Physical descriptions of people. Quite detailed. Like a diary which contains essentially the skeleton of information. The first entry reads: 'Tall chestnut-haired man on south-west corner of Fifty-Seventh and Sixth. I thought he smiled at me. Was probably wiping a speck of dirt from the corner of his mouth.' The last entry: 'Pretty redhead, five-three, in elevator at Chrysler Building. I sneezed. She didn't notice.' (*Beat.*) I have never seen anything like his closet. An enormous walk-in inside which was all the furniture. An EZ chair. A captain's chair. A chipped maple bureau. An oak schoolboy's desk. An Army issue wool blanket. Three goose-down pillows. And framed family photographs. Except on closer inspection, we discover they are the photographs that came with the frames. One frame still carried its price sticker. And there are very few articles of clothing. Almost none. (*Beat.*) The bathroom is spotless. So is the kitchen. We find nothing. No hair. No fingerprints. Certainly, most certainly, we find no blood. In the medicine cabinet there's a four-year-old empty prescription bottle of Tylenol with codeine. On the fridge is taped a postcard of Napoleon's tomb. Postmarked at the GPO on Thirty-Third and Eighth. It's addressed to Elston and carries no message. Inside the fridge, one mouldy grapefruit. One unopened box of Devil Dogs. An eight-ounce can of Campbell's V-8 juice. An airline-sized bottle of Stolichnaya vodka. (*Beat.*) The only eating utensils are plastic. Four knives, two forks, seven spoons, neatly stacked in a plastic cutlery tray. Two plastic dinner plates. One ceramic coffee mug. One soup bowl, badly chipped. A broken two-slice toaster. A roulette wheel ashtray from Resorts International, Atlantic City. A Manhattan residential telephone directory in which are circled in red felt pen the numbers of well-known people. He has no telephone, but he has written a listing for himself in the directory. He wrote it in black ink.

An uncomfortable silence.

Ellen   So, officer, this is very interesting and all, but I don't see why you gotta tell us the contents of this creep's refrigerator. My baby girl is dead and you're telling me about tomato juice?

Ted   In going over the details, there is the possibility of finding clues.

Anthony   Where's this guy now? He's out on the street? You let him go?

Ted   He's co-operated. He *asked* us to examine his apartment. He's told us his version of events, which does not differ significantly from Jack Fallon's version of events. Except, of course, that Elston Rupp does not recall Jack Fallon's self-confessed heroics.

Anthony   So this guy, this little fuck, he's out and walking around?

Ted   Would you like me to arrest him for impersonating an entertainment attorney?

Ellen HE MURDERED MY DAUGHTER. DROWNED HER IN A BATHTUB.

Ted We have nothing to substantiate that.

Ellen Yeah, well, you got nothing that doesn't prove it, do you?

Ted I don't know what to tell you.

Anthony You believe this guy?

Ted I am tending toward it, yes.

Ellen You believe this faggot psycho who walks around in dirty clothes but you don't believe normal people like us?

Ted You weren't there. He was. Listen to me. I would bet that if you rounded up, at random, two or three dozen guys who live in a ten-block radius, you'd find that they'd all tell more or less the same sad story. The exact same story of their lives, Mrs Casey. The details would not significantly differ from man to man.

Anthony I got a friend, this guy I grew up with in Bay Ridge? Since he was a kid, he's been collecting his girlfriends' toe-nail clippings. Can you imagine? Puts them in a shoebox.

Ellen Whatsa matter with you, Anthony? You taking his side? You taking the side of a pervert?

Anthony Mrs Casey, no offence. You know, it's just – some guys, they're weird.

Ted Yes. Some guys are weird.

Ellen I'm sitting here with a couple of professional fucking Freuds and neither of them can tell me what's happened to my daughter.

Ted Perhaps she did simply leave. Go away. Escape.

Ellen My daughter would never ESCAPE. She wasn't the type. Besides, she was gonna get married. She was gonna go to Sicily on her honeymoon. We was all gonna go. Personally, I wasn't big on the idea of Italy. But at my age, I'd take anything. Right, Anthony?

Anthony   Mrs Casey, she didn't wanna marry me. I mean, we gotta give her some due. The girl said she did not want to marry me.

Ted   Is that true, Mrs Casey?

Ellen   What does he know? What? He cuts hair for a living. That's not normal. My daughter, she – oh what's the point. She was fucked up. That's the point. I don't care. I don't. Whether she's dead or gone to New Jersey or if she's camped out on the ROOF. I DON'T CARE.

Another uncomfortable silence.

Ted   There won't be an arrest. I'm sorry. I think that Sarah is alive. I hope . . . you get a phone call or a note that says, hi Mom. I've decided to become a Shaker and I'm making furniture in Pennsylvania. (*Beat.*) I have nothing else to offer at the moment.

Ellen   Hey, hey – WAIT. You can't go. Where's my satisfaction? Huh? WHAT AM I LEFT WITH?

Ted   I don't know. Another blanket?

Ted *exits.* **Ellen** *holds up the unfinished blanket.*

Ellen   I called my daughter a booze-bag. That's the last thing I said to her.

Ellen *cries.* **Anthony** *tries to dry her tears away with the blanket.*

Twelve

Elston *and* **Natalie** *at the police station.*

Elston   Thank you for coming. Are you mad at me?

Natalie   Why would I be mad at you?

Elston   A day's revenue. Lost.

Natalie   Well. You'll make it up to me.

Elston   How?

Natalie (*after a beat*)   Elston. Is everything, well, is it all okay now? Did you – fix it?

Elston   I'm not arrested. If that's what you mean.

Natalie   Good. I'm glad it's over.

Elston   It's not over. There's the girl.

Natalie   Of course. The girl. (*Beat.*) We can't help that, Elston. We don't know where she is.

Elston   Yes, we do.

Natalie   We do?

Elston   Yes. She's elsewhere. (*Beat.*) Are you going to fire me?

Natalie   Probably not.

Elston   Are you going to give me a raise?

Natalie   No. Well. Eventually.

Elston   That's okay. I don't need money.

Natalie   Elston, everybody needs money.

Elston   I used to think so. (*Beat.*) I had some people over at my apartment this morning.

Natalie   I wasn't aware you had any friends.

Elston   I don't. They were detectives. Men with magnifying glasses.

Natalie   Oh. That must have been exciting. Or something.

Elston   I invited them. But I shouldn't have.

Natalie   I imagine they would have invited themselves into your apartment if you hadn't extended the courtesy.

Elston   That's an odd concept. Extending courtesy. Like extending a hand. (*Beat.*) Do you know where I live?

Natalie   Uhm. No. Yes, yes – I mean, I read about it. In the *Post*. But your address wasn't given out. Not exactly.

Elston   Too bad.

Natalie   Why would you want a bunch of strangers knowing your address?

Elston   You're not a stranger. (*Beat.*) I live on the highway. Well. Above the highway. In a room. I can see the traffic.

Natalie   That's . . . pleasant.

Elston   I watch the traffic and think, where are you all going? Why don't you stop a while? Slow down. And then I realize I shouldn't be concerned about speeding cars when I don't even know who my neighbours are. Or if I even have any neighbours. My building might very well be deserted. Except for me.

Natalie   People make noise. They cook. You'd know if they were there.

Elston   I don't cook.

Natalie   Well. Neither do I. So. There you go.

Elston   Let me take you to dinner.

Natalie   No. I can't. I have . . . a friend. From out of town. Visiting.

Elston   Oh. A traveller.

Natalie   Why don't you see a movie?

Elston   I don't see movies.

Natalie   Oh, come on. An insignificant little comedy, something to take your mind off –

Elston   Nothing is insignificant. (*Beat.*) What an interesting phrase: take one's mind off. Have you ever noticed how most of the language we use to suggest mental activity conjures up a violent physical action? Take one's mind off. Off his rocker. (*Beat.*) I have to go home now. I have to watch traffic.

Natalie   Elston, I've got to ask you a really big favour. I know you've got a load on your – what I mean is. Well, would you please not wear the customers' clothes any more? I don't want to be a bitch, but. It's probably unsanitary.

Elston   Give and take.

Natalie If it was up to me, I would let you borrow . . . whatever . . . you know.

Elston It is up to you.

Natalie The customers are horrified.

Elston How do you know? You're never there. (*Beat.*) The favour. What's the favour you want?

Natalie That. I just asked you. About the clothes.

Elston Don't you want me to buy you groceries? Or flowers?

Natalie I hate flowers. And I don't cook. Remember?

Elston I might move to New Jersey.

Natalie Why would you do that? It's across the river.

Elston Well. You won't allow me to offer you any courtesy. But I can offer you my hand.

Elston *extends his hand to* **Natalie**.

Natalie Elston. This is a little weird, isn't it?

Elston We're friends.

Natalie We . . . know each other. A bit. Yes.

Elston Shake my hand. Please.

Natalie (*after a beat*) I'll see you tomorrow. At the shop. Don't be ridiculous.

Elston *drops his hand.*

Elston You've been very kind. I think. I – I'll open the shop early tomorrow. I'll make it up to you. I think. I think – good night. Natalie.

Natalie Yes. Uhm. Ciao.

Elston *exits.* **Natalie** *lights a cigarette. She doesn't smoke it.* **Ted** *enters.*

Natalie I meant to be nice to him. Take him to dinner. Buy him a drink. Something. But I couldn't. He. He makes my skin crawl.

Thirteen

Jack *and* **Timothy** *at O'Malley's Saloon.*

Timothy   I had to see it. For myself. I hope you don't mind.

Jack   No skin off my back, bud.

Timothy   It's hard to believe, but I've never been this far west.

Jack   Yeah? Do you like it?

Timothy   I've lived in New York eighteen years and I've never seen this part of town. I imagined, I don't know, something different.

Jack   Yeah. I know. People think all sorts of things. Tough things.

Timothy   Show me where she sat.

Jack   Huh?

Timothy   Sarah Casey. That night. Where did she sit?

Jack (*indicating the barstool*)   It ain't a shrine, mister.

Timothy (*sits on the barstool*)   Did she sit like this?

Jack   Yeah. I guess. To tell you the truth, it's kinda fuzzy to me now.

Timothy   And Rupp. Where did he sit?

Jack   Someplace else. I don't know. Funny how your memory goes, real quick like.

Timothy   They walked out that door together. And Sarah Casey was never seen again. Rupp touched that doorknob. The night appeared. And she was gone. (*Beat.*) I dream about this.

Jack   Lemme give you some advice, pal. Forget it. You wasn't even here. Me, now I was here. And I can't even remember where the fuck they sat. It's better that way.

Timothy   Better for whom?

Jack   You got to grab your bull by its horns. Like me. Take me, right? I'm buying a new sign, some of that fancy neon. I call the bar Sarah Casey's now. Didya know that?

Timothy   Well. Congratulations.

Jack   I figure, Sarah, she was a tough kid. She woulda appreciated my business sense. She's gone, it don't matter. She comes back, she'll be honoured to have the place named after her.

Timothy   A beacon on the highway.

Jack   Huh?

Timothy   A candle in the window.

Jack   Yeah, sure. Candles in windows. That's good. I might do that. Like I said, you gotta figure your angle on every situation. What's your angle on this, mister?

Timothy   I'm in therapy.

Jack   Whoa, buddy. Heavy shit.

Timothy   Don't you think your life has been altered in some way? I mean, I might be having dinner with my kids now. But I'm not. You might be shooting the shit with Sarah Casey now. If not for this.

Jack   Nope. I think . . . we're doing exactly what we're meant to be doing. And I think there's reasons for what we're doing but fuck me if I know what they are.

Timothy   Has business picked up since – since the, uh, name change?

Jack   Nah. But it could. I betcha it could.

Timothy   Elston Rupp. That's one of those names. A name from another universe.

Jack   Yeah. A real . . . farmer name.

Timothy (*after a beat*)   I'd like a drink.

Jack   Sure. Listen, it's on me. What'll you have?

Timothy   Stoly Martini. Olives. (*Beat.*) Did you really make Rupp for a killer when he walked through that door.

Jack   Personally, between me and you – this is between me and you, right?

Timothy   Right.

Jack   Look, I couldn't tell a killer from a fucking priest. But Rupp's not talking and she's not here, right?

Timothy   Right.

Jack   But I did win the Golden Gloves. I swear.

Fourteen

Elston *and* **Ted** *at the thrift shop.* **Ted** *carries a box of clothing.*

Ted   I've brought some things.

Elston   Are they clean?

Ted   I washed them myself. Ironed everything. Even the socks.

Elston   Why?

Ted   Why not?

Elston   I mean, why here? Don't you have a local thrift shop?

Ted   I want to keep in touch.

Elston   You feel you know me.

Ted   I don't know you.

Elston   You've dusted my apartment for fingerprints. You feel you're entitled.

Ted   Look. I'm just donating some clothes. I'm sorry.

Elston   I'm sorry for you. Are you sorry for me?

Ted   I'm troubled by you.

Elston   I burned my notepads. You read them.

Ted   I browsed through them.

Elston   Why didn't you read them?

Ted   It wasn't necessary.

Elston   It was necessary. If you wanted to know me. But you don't. So.

Ted   There are unresolved questions. I'd like to ask you. But.

Elston   I won't answer your questions any more, Ted. Because if I answered them, you wouldn't come back here.

Ted   If you answer me, I won't bother you again.

Elston   Bother me, Ted. (*Beat.*) I hope Sarah Casey's in Winchester.

Ted   So do I.

Elston   People from all over the city come in here just to look at me. Do you think they're afraid of me?

Ted   Do they look you in the eye?

Elston   Never. I had this thought yesterday: before Sarah Casey disappeared, I probably stood a better chance of making eye contact with a person, even though I was anonymous. Now. Well. I couldn't tell you the eye colour of anybody who's been here in the last week. (*Beat.*) You don't look me in the eye, Ted.

Ted   Maybe you should get another job.

Elston   Do you think I could be a detective?

Ted   Well, if you can't stand people fearing you, then police work is not ideal.

Elston   I didn't say I couldn't stand it. You can't stand it, though. (*Beat.*) I don't see Natalie any more. She has a messenger pick up the week's receipts on Sunday nights. The messenger brings me my paycheck. There's a different messenger each week. So there's some variety. I see more people that way.

Ted   You watched that woman walk away. Tell me you watched her walk away.

Elston   Last week, the messenger asked me for my autograph. It was thrilling. But he thought I was the lawyer. He thought I was Timothy Creighton.

Ted   Verify it for me. Please.

Elston   There's some irony in this, Ted.

Ted   People just don't disappear.

Elston   I know that. (*Beat.*) You'll need a receipt. For the clothes.

Ted   Maybe you're right. I should bring them someplace closer to home.

Elston   I knew you weren't the type to give away your old clothes. You hoard things. People. Faces. You can't stand the thought of other people in your pants.

Ted   I'll go now.

Elston   I thrive on all things second-hand.

Ted   Well. I guess that's why you like me. (*Beat.*) Goodbye, Elston.

Elston   You'll come back.

Ted   Anything's possible.

Elston   You're mine.

Ted *exits, leaving his clothes behind.* **Elston** *begins to undress.*

Elston   I can't wear clothes at all any more. I'm doing this favour for Natalie.

Fifteen

At O'Malley's. **Elston**, **Sarah** *and* **Jack**, *as in Scene One. Music in: 'Happy Together' (The Turtles).*

Elston   The fascinating thing about being an entertainment attorney is that you meet people who have problems you couldn't begin to imagine. It makes one feel better about one's own problems.

Sarah   I don't guess you have many problems. You have money.

Elston   I carry the burden of all my clients' sadness.

Sarah   That is such bullshit. You hear this guy, Jack? He's talking about carrying burdens.

Jack   Burdens are what animals carry.

Elston   I'm an animal. Aren't you an animal, Jack?

Jack   Hey, I like animals. But I ain't no animal.

Elston   It would be simpler. To be an animal.

Jack   You couldn't protect yourself. You'd be at the mercy of other animals. Bigger animals.

Elston   What if you had teeth? And say you were seven feet tall. You couldn't think, certainly. But you could protect yourself. Seeking protection is a primary animal instinct.

Sarah   I wanna be a fish. Then I could swim. A lot.

Elston   You could swim away. The earth, Sarah Casey, is seventy-five per cent water. And so are we.

Sarah   Yeah, but I'd wanna be a slim fish. A pretty fish. And that way, I wouldn't last long. I'd get eaten up in a hurry. Or else end up in some sadistic kid's fish tank.

Elston   Why does the kid have to be sadistic?

Sarah   Well. Let's just say it's my burden.

Jack   I hadda mute parrot when I was a kid. Christ. I wish I'd tortured it.

Sarah   Oh, man. I really really wanna get out of here.

Elston   People always say 'I wanna get out'. And they rarely mean it. They rarely walk away. We stay. We don't take steps.

Sarah   That's easy for you to say, Mister-Entertainment-Attorney-to-the-Stars.

Elston What if I told you that I live in one room. That I use no furniture. That I sleep in a closet. Would you believe me?

Sarah Whaddya think, Jack? You believe this guy sleeps in a closet?

Jack No way. This guy, he sleeps on a fucking king-sized waterbed.

Sarah Yeah. And he's got some obnoxious bitch wife who spends all his money. And he loves it.

Elston I like the bit about the money. Go on.

Jack He's got a Swiss bank account. And he . . . collects. Yeah, he collects like, mink stoles. Sells them to the Japs.

Elston Ermine. It would have to be ermine.

Sarah He's got a castle in Germany. On the Rhine. That's a river, Jack. And he wants to teach his wife how to waltz, but she's too pigheaded to learn. It frustrates him. A lot.

Elston That's perfect. So far.

Sarah So. He likes to dance and he would love to learn Greek, but his fucking mother is always criticizing him about it. Constant ridicule. He doesn't have any close friends. And he's trapped in this loveless marriage he doesn't have a clue how to get out of.

Elston And what does he do about this?

Sarah He . . . doesn't know. He feels like a fake, like he's not entitled to something different because he doesn't have any money.

Elston But he has a castle on the Rhine.

Sarah Right. But it's . . . it's his mother's castle. She's evil and she won't give him NOTHING. And he he he – lives in one room with a a a single bed and a desk with nothing in it and her only hope the only piece of comfort she has is a stupid old record nailed to her stupid old wall which is painted pink 'cause her bitch of a mother says pink is for

GIRLS and she clings to this delusion that the record was
written for her and she thinks that means she's entitled to
GO SOMEWHERE SHE'S NEVER BEEN. (*Beat.*) Which,
for her, is just about everywhere. She knows the name of
practically every shit hole in this wide wide world but she's
only seen the names on maps. She'll probably marry a good-
natured man who she won't love, because at least then she
can take a vacation. But basically, she thinks she'll drink
until she drops.

Elston   And then?

Sarah   Something endless and black. She'll have a kid
'cause she's got nothing better to do. She'll be tempted to
drown the kid, but she won't. Because she is not an animal,
even though maybe she would like to be a fish. But she can't
swim. 'Cause she never learned.

Elston   And then, having no other option, she will walk on
air.

Sarah   He's talking shit again, Jack. Just when I was
beginning to like him a little.

Elston   I'm talking about miracles, Sarah. Our capacity to
accept the impossible increases exponentially when we are at
the ends of our ropes. (*Beat.*) Are you really beginning to like
me?

Sarah   I got a soft spot for religious fanatics.

Elston   Have you ever been at the end of your rope, Sarah?

Sarah   Sure. Can't you see my rope burns?

Elston   I have them, too.

Sarah   Yeah. Well. We can march in a parade some day
and reminisce about our war wounds.

Elston   I can walk on air.

Sarah   God. I wish that was true. I do.

Elston   If I could walk on air, it would be the most strange
and wondrous sight, no?

Jack The strangest thing I ever seen was my mother burying this mouse she killed in a trap. She breaks the thing's neck, right? And then she goes all soft and wants to bury it in the fucking backyard. And get this, like, she wants to dress it up in something nice. And the only nice thing she's got is my christening robe. I say, ma, whaddya wacko or something? And she says, Jack, it'd be a sin not to bury this mouse in a soft white robe and since you just too dumb to have kids, I don't expect you'll be needing it. (*Beat.*) And I had to agree with her.

Sarah Thank you, Jack. You've proved once and for all that it's possible for men to walk on air. Thank you.

Elston What's the strangest thing you've ever seen, Sarah?

Sarah Well. Aside from the sight of me in my mother's house? Let's see. I'd have to say . . . this guy. He comes into the travel shop a couple of weeks ago. He's got this map in his pocket. The map's so old and so worn it looks like it's come outta the womb with this guy. He asks me to close my eyes and pick a vacation destination for him off this map. But it's a map of the tri-state metropolitan area. He insists I choose. And so. I close my eyes and I pick the Holland Tunnel. This guy is so . . . so grateful. His desire to go anywhere – just to go – is so strong. So well-defined. He has such trust. In me. And suddenly I feel the desire to kiss him, full on the lips, for a very long time. Because really, he has as little idea of where to go or what to do as I have. I don't kiss him. I don't take him by his hand and lead him into the world. I am eyeball to eyeball with a man who's the only person I'm likely to meet who fully understands the desire to simply . . . vanish. And I send him into a tunnel.

Elston That's the saddest story I've ever heard.

Sarah I know. Don't you think I know that?

Elston Maybe you'll meet that man again. And you'll walk on air. Together.

Sarah I wouldn't know him if he bit me in the ass.

Elston   You can make the choice to remember. I do. You can take steps. What do you think, Jack? Can you take steps?

Jack   Yeah, sure. I step outta my apartment, I step outta my car, I step in my bar, I step back out to my car, I step back into my apartment. Lotta steps, I'm taking.

Sarah   Look. It's been nice, guys. But. Time to face the music. Time for beddie-bye. Time to imagine myself falling asleep to something other than the sounds of hookers getting pissed on the highway.

Elston   The waves lapping gently past your castle on the Rhine.

Sarah   Sure. Fairy tales do come true it can happen to you. If you're deluded at heart. (*Beat.*) I'm so . . . something . . . I can't even push myself to walk. I gotta stop drinking and start walking.

Elston   Let me help you to the door. I have a long walk ahead of me. It's time I started off.

Jack   That's a fuck of a long walk, mister, to the East Side.

Elston   Not if you walk on air.

Sarah   Whaddya think, Jack? Am I stepping out with a lawyer or with some maniac who drowns women in his bathtub?

Jack *shrugs.*

Elston (*as he opens the door*)   Does it matter, Sarah Casey?

Sarah (*a beat, as she considers this*)   Makes no difference to me. But I sure hope you do walk on air. 'Cause it would be something to see.

Elston   Our potential to walk on air is infinite. Shall we?

Elston *bows to* **Sarah** *as he holds the door open for her.* **Sarah** *exits. A beat, then* **Elston** *follows her out, the door remaining open behind him.*

Blackout.

Methuen Modern Plays

include work by

Jean Anouilh
John Arden
Margaretta D'Arcy
Peter Barnes
Sebastian Barry
Brendan Behan
Edward Bond
Bertolt Brecht
Howard Brenton
Simon Burke
Jim Cartwright
Caryl Churchill
Noël Coward
Sarah Daniels
Nick Dear
Shelagh Delaney
David Edgar
Dario Fo
Michael Frayn
John Godber
Paul Godfrey
John Guare
Peter Handke
Jonathan Harvey
Iain Heggie
Declan Hughes
Terry Johnson
Barrie Keeffe
Stephen Lowe

Doug Lucie
John McGrath
David Mamet
Patrick Marber
Arthur Miller
Mtwa, Ngema & Simon
Tom Murphy
Phyllis Nagy
Peter Nichols
Joseph O'Connor
Joe Orton
Louise Page
Luigi Pirandello
Stephen Poliakoff
Franca Rame
Philip Ridley
David Rudkin
Willy Russell
Jean-Paul Sartre
Sam Shepard
Wole Soyinka
C. P. Taylor
Theatre de Complicite
Theatre Workshop
Sue Townsend
Judy Upton
Timberlake Wertenbaker
Victoria Wood

Methuen World Classics

Aeschylus (two volumes)
Jean Anouilh
John Arden (two volumes)
Arden & D'Arcy
Aristophanes (two volumes)
Aristophanes & Menander
Peter Barnes (two volumes)
Brendan Behan
Aphra Behn
Edward Bond (four volumes)
Bertolt Brecht
  (five volumes)
Howard Brenton
  (two volumes)
Büchner
Bulgakov
Calderón
Anton Chekhov
Caryl Churchill
  (two volumes)
Noël Coward (five volumes)
Sarah Daniels (two volumes)
Eduardo De Filippo
David Edgar (three volumes)
Euripides (three volumes)
Dario Fo (two volumes)
Michael Frayn (two volumes)
Max Frisch
Gorky
Harley Granville Barker
  (two volumes)
Henrik Ibsen (six volumes)

Terry Johnson
Lorca (three volumes)
David Mamet
Marivaux
Mustapha Matura
David Mercer (two volumes)
Arthur Miller
  (five volumes)
Anthony Minghella
Molière
Tom Murphy
  (three volumes)
Musset
Peter Nichols (two volumes)
Clifford Odets
Joe Orton
Louise Page
A. W. Pinero
Luigi Pirandello
Stephen Poliakoff
  (two volumes)
Terence Rattigan
Ntozake Shange
Sophocles (two volumes)
Wole Soyinka
David Storey (two volumes)
August Strindberg
  (three volumes)
J. M. Synge
Ramón del Valle-Inclán
Frank Wedekind
Oscar Wilde

Royal Court Writers

The Royal Court Writers series was launched in 1981 to celebrate 25 years of the English Stage company and 21 years since the publication of the first Methuen Modern Play. Published to coincide with each production, the series fulfils the dual role of programme and playscript.

The Royal Court Writers Series includes work by

Karim Alrawi
Thomas Babe
Sebastian Barry
Neil Bartlett
Aphra Behn
Howard Brenton
Jim Cartwright
Anton Chekhov
Caryl Churchill
Sarah Daniels
George Farquhar
John Guare
Iain Heggie
Robert Holman
Ron Hutchinson

Terry Johnson
Manfred Karge
Charlotte Keatley
Paul Kember
Hanif Kureishi
Stephen Lowe
David Mamet
Mariane Mayer
G. F. Newman
Wallace Shawn
Sam Shepard
David Storey
Sue Townsend
Timberlake Wertenbaker
Snoo Wilson

New titles also available from Methuen

John Godber
Lucky Sods & Passion Killers
0 413 70170 0

Paul Godfrey
A Bucket of Eels & The Modern Husband
0 413 68830 5

Jonathan Harvey
Boom Bang-A-Bang & Rupert Street Lonely Hearts Club
0 413 70450 5

Judy Upton
Bruises & The Shorewatchers' House
0 413 70430 0

For a Complete Catalogue of Methuen Drama titles
write to:

Methuen Drama
Michelin House
81 Fulham Road
London SW3 6RB

Lightning Source UK Ltd.
Milton Keynes UK
UKOW02f0823121215